...EDITION
...Printing, 1992

...photo: Frank Dorland
...design: Terry Buske
...ations: Charles T. Smith, Brooke Luteyn, and
...elen Byers

...y of Congress Cataloging-in-Publication Data
...man, Catherine, 1953—
...ystal Awareness

...ewellyn's new age series)
... Quartz crystals—Miscellanea. 2. Occultism.
...ealing—Miscellanea I Title.   II. Series
...42.Q35B68 1987   133   87–46112
...N 0–87542–058–3 (pbk)

...llyn Publications
...ision of Llewellyn Worldwide, Ltd.
...ox 64383, St. Paul, MN 55164-0383

P9-DEQ-532

About the Author

Catherine Bowman was initiated into metaphysics by her parents while she was quite young. She earned university degrees in psychology and education, and has worked for a major Canadian telecommunications company. At 32, she reached a crossroads as to her goals and direction in life. After much soul searching and a powerful experience with Anna Mitchell Hedge's Crystal Skull, she chose the spiritual path, resulting in a positive, new self-image.

She left her job in order to write a simple, practical guide for those people just starting to work with crystal energies in order to help advance their self-awareness. The project led her to study under Dr. Frank Alper, becoming a Spiritual Healer and Counselor certified through his Arizona Metaphysical Society.

To Write to the Author

We cannot guarantee that every letter written to the author can be answered, but all will be forwarded. Both the author and the publisher appreciate hearing from readers, learning of your enjoyment and benefit from this book. Llewellyn also publishes a bi-monthly news magazine with news and reviews of practical esoteric studies and articles helpful to the student, and some readers' questions and comments to the author may be answered through this magazine's columns if permission to do is included in the original letter. The author sometimes participates in seminars and workshops, and dates and places are announced in *The Llewellyn New Times*. To write to the author, or to ask a question, write to:

Catherine Bowman
c/o THE LLEWELLYN NEW TIMES
P.O. Box 64383-058, St. Paul, MN 55164-0383, U.S.A.
Please enclose a self-addressed, stamped envelope for reply, or $1.00
to cover costs.

Llewellyn's New Age S

CRYSTA AWAREND

By

Catherine Bown

1992
Llewellyn Publications
St. Paul, Minnesota 55164–03

ABOUT LLEWELLYN'S NEW AGE SERIES

The "New Age"—it's a phrase we use, but what does it mean? Does it mean that we are entering the Aquarian Age? Does it mean that a new Messiah is coming to correct all that is wrong and make Earth into a Garden? Probably not—but the idea of a *major change* is there, combined with awareness that Earth *can* be a Garden; that war, crime, poverty, disease, etc., are not necessary "evils."

Optimists, dreamers, scientists . . . nearly all of us believe in a "better tomorrow," and that somehow we can do things now that will make for a better future life for ourselves and for coming generations.

In one sense, we all know there's nothing new under the Heavens, and in another sense that every day makes a new world. The difference is in our consciousness. And this is what the New Age is all about: it's a major change in consciousness found within each of us as we learn to bring forth and manifest powers that Humanity has always potentially had.

Evolution moves in "leaps." Individuals struggle to develop talents and powers, and their efforts build a "power bank" in the Collective Unconsciousness, the "soul" of Humanity that suddenly makes these same talents and powers easier access for the majority.

You still have to learn the 'rules' for developing and applying these powers, but it is more like a "relearning" than a *new* learning, because with the New Age it is as if the basis for these had become genetic.

Forthcoming book from Catherine Bowman

Advancing Awareness

*Dedicated in light and love
to Raouf and the eternal vibrations
of Adamis and Mathos.*

THIS IS MY TRUTH

.

Toronto
September, 1986

CONTENTS

Foreword

For many years psychics have been predicting the "rising of Atlantis." It has, in reality, taken place many years ago in the form of energy and knowledge now available to mankind.

We have become aware of crystals and more crystals. We have been channeled methodology of geometric patterns and applications for many purposes, i.e. healing, channeling, communication and education.

Crystals are not a "New Age fad," nor are they toys. They are real and will serve mankind for generations to come. What an exciting future awaits us as we begin to open our minds to the realities of magnetic energy and how it will drastically alter our lives in the future.

In my travels throughout the world, I find more and more people opening their minds to holistic living and the utilization of crystals in their lives. It shows us that we are growing and becoming receptive to higher, ancient patterns of energy and knowledge.

Because crystals absorb energy patterns, they are capable of serving our stated needs. For example, if we wish to use them to emanate blue light, we merely need to hold the crystal in our hand, have a thought in our mind, and the blue frequency will be drawn into the crystal for our use and dissemination.

Crystals have been used on Earth for over 80,000 years. They were the source of power in the ancient civilizations of Lemuria and Atlantis. They were used as conductors of energy information from the civilizations to other forms of conscious expression of life.

Realizing that geometrics was the language of the Universe (it is without distortion), the Atlanteans developed patterns that created numerous forcefields of energy to serve a wide spectrum of needs. All of this information has gradually been coming into conscious awareness on Earth for the past ten years.

We have a great responsibility here on Earth. We must express great care and concern for the proper usage of these energies and information. Crystals are not to be used for "fun and games," or to be taken too lightly. The energies are real. We have used them in radios, watches, computers and many other instruments available to us at this time. You should seek information about them and learn to use them properly. In this manner, the knowledge will continue to be made available to us in the coming years.

You are as a crystal-pure energy that vibrates with your Universe. You can resonate with all the knowledge of eternity. Your crystal will amplify this knowledge for you until the day comes when you are as one with this energy. Then you have become master of yourself and an enlightened being.

In crystal Light and Love,
Dr. Frank Alper

Introduction

Time and time again I come.
Time and time I am refused the entrance.
I cannot get in.
I know not why I am blocked.

—Dea

People are beginning to seek answers to their questions of why life is so complex and why our current civilization has degenerated into a mass of contradictions. When philosophy, psychology, self-help groups, and even religion fail to provide meaningful outward solutions, people begin to search within. An entrance may be accessed into this inner conscious awareness through the use of quartz crystals.

This book combines the author's own inner truth with her research and experimentation to provide the reader with the basic ground rules for working with quartz crystals. The information is principally directed toward those people who are starting to use crystal energies.

The main focus of the book is on personal development through crystal meditations and healing arrangements. Simple illustrated instructions are used throughout to avoid any possibility of confusion.

It is the author's intention to enable the reader

to bypass the bewilderment and mistakes usually encountered in the beginning stages of crystal work. Hopefully, the reader will be stimulated to create personal growth techniques while gaining an appreciation for the infinite capabilities of crystal* energies.

---

*The word crystal denotes quartz unless otherwise indicated.

1

THE NEW ENERGY

A new level of energy has been accumulating on this planet since the late 1970's. Both mankind and the Earth are experiencing its effects.

March of 1985* witnessed the retreat of the Piscean Age of Reasoning with the arrival of the Age of Aquarius. This is believed to be the long awaited era of Enlightenment bringing knowledge, understanding and peace to our world. Instead, the opposite appears to be occurring. Today's highly acclaimed technology along with geological changes (thought to be caused by a shifting of the Earth's axis) are combining to create an increasing number of earthquakes, volcanic eruptions and other natural disasters. Our current lack of cohesion among people is producing political upheavals, terrorism, and global unrest. Our planet seems to be on a course of self-destruction.

This new energy does, however, have a posi-

*From the channeling of Dr. Frank Alper, Arizona Metaphysical Society.

tive side. It is creating a growing awareness among an increasing number of people. These are the emerging Aquarian Children of Light sharing their knowledge, love and hope to counterbalance the mounting negative aspects of our world. This New Age has reintroduced the apparently unlimited powers of quartz crystal to help these people in their arduous task.

Crystals are all around us. Some authorities believe that nearly thirty-three percent of the Earth's surface is composed of this mineral, while unknown quantities lie beneath her waters. The general population is taking notice of these stones as evidenced by the growing number of crystals and related materials found in rock shops, jewelry, books and workshops.

In the legendary civilizations of Atlantis and Lemuria, crystals were the basic energy source as well as being used for healing, teaching and interstellar communication. In more recent times, shamans utilized these stones in ceremonial rites to link man with his spirits. Alchemists worked with the hidden properties of crystals to unlock the secrets of the Earth. Crystal balls are still being used by seers and psychics attempting to tap into the outer dimensions of time and space.

Uses in Technology

Crystals are at work in many ways, affecting our modern life. They are used in watches, appliances, radios, televisions, computers and telecommunication equipment.

Two of the best known qualities contained in quartz are its piezoelectrical effects and memory capacity in silicon chips. It was discovered that an electrical current was induced by mechanically squeezing a thin wafer of crystal. Also, when an electrical current was applied to a section of quartz cut to a specific size, a fixed vibrational frequency or oscillation resulted.

In the late 1940's, researchers found that by adding foreign atoms to the crystal, a transmitting device could be made. This was used in radios which amplified the electrical signals, sending them to the piezoelectric crystal which in turn vibrated, creating sound. This invention of the transmitter rendered vacuum tubes obsolete. Transmitters open the door to modern telecommunications equipment with their use in electrical items such as radios, televisions, and mainframe computers.

For several years, information (including the human voice) needed to be converted into an electrical wave called an *analog* before it could be transmitted. In the last two decades, the transmitter evolved into digital computer technology. Today, information is coded into the language of computers for fast, accurate transmission. This was made possible through the discovery of silicon chips made from quartz, which have the capacity to store, receive and transmit. These chips, integrated circuits or semi-conductors convert analog to digital and back again, putting information into any type of receiving equipment. Without quartz, we would not have mini or micro computers, electronic office equipment, microwave controls, electronic automobile ignitions, electronic cash registers, and other time-saving devices that we have come to rely and depend upon. And, we are only at the beginning . . .

Crystals have an even greater importance than their use in our state-of-the-art technology. They are here to help us rise above the monotony and limits of our present life by providing access to the inner dimensions of the mind.

The vast majority of mankind has been historically confined to a three-dimensional world. Until the nineteenth century, existence revolved around the full time work of providing food, shelter and clothing. Mind expansion and development was left to the few who had these basic essentials provided. Physically, the twentieth century progressed us from the agrarian and industrial eras into the fast-paced world of technology. Spiritually, this New Age is awakening our inner latent talents and abilities by invoking the need for personal development.

Due to today's increased stress, the need for material possessions, disintegrating relationships and lack of personal space, many people are being forced to search within themselves for the inner sanctuary of conscious awareness.

Definition of Awareness

Most of us understand the word *conscious*. We are consciously aware of our body's external physical surroundings of daily routines and activities. The word *awareness* denotes being attentive, perceptive, sensitive and in tune with our internal self. But to be *consciously aware* takes us one step further, for it implies a sensitivity to external as well as internal conditions. It is a knowingness, an understanding and recognition of both the subconscious and conscious states. Most conflicts in life are due to a barrier between these two expressions which can be as different as night and day. The subconscious intuitive self is disregarded as being illogical, while the conscious thinking state is socially acceptable. We have suppressed our intuitive faculties which are totally devoid of reasoning and logic, and unaffected by the physical senses. This astonishing capacity to forewarn, foretell, and guide our conscious thoughts lies relatively untapped, awaiting to be released. Crystals can help to liberate these areas of the mind and enable us to maintain a heightened balance between the subconscious and conscious states.

To date, there is no hard scientific, medical or psychological evidence to corroborate the fact that crystals help to raise conscious awareness. Our scientific measuring tools are still too primitive. Instead, it is a private personal confirmation, a knowingness of being in balance with all aspects of the self that reveal how crystals assist us.

Generally, the best crystals to be used for this expansion of awareness are natural, unpolished, colorless quartz. These minerals can best be described as living computers with none of the human impediments of emotion, prejudice, judgement or skepticism. They are always ready, willing and able to perform a programmed task. As multi-purpose tools, they never wear out and have no moving or replacement parts.

Crystals are here to teach and serve us. To the awakening mind, they are capable of performing a multitude of functions such as dream guidance and direction, cleansing the body of negative energies, focusing the mind, mental and physical healing, telepathy, linkages to special places, and other potentially limitless tasks.

Welcome to the Crystal Age of Aquarius, the dawn of your awakening. With patience, determination, hard work and belief in your own inherent abilities, crystals can help to accelerate and direct this inner development. Perhaps this planet can be returned to its original balanced state through each individual gaining an understanding of self, then sharing this inner truth and knowledge with others.

2

CRYSTAL FORMS

While a stone to the touch,
it seems like water to the eye.
— St. Jerome

A triangle represents the universal building block from which all geometric shapes (including the circle and square) are derived. The quantum building block of quartz crystal is a three-sided pyramid composed of equilateral triangles. This shape is also one of the most important expressions of the Law of Three.*

Only an interaction between three forces can create movement. "According to many ancient systems, all phenomena that exist from the gods downward arise from an interaction of three forces."[1] If only two forces were present, there would be a perfect balance with no movement. The introduction of a third force produces a reaction in the

---

*One of the many Universal Laws that govern our lives. They cannot be scientifically proven, nor can they be seen. They are just *experienced.* Another example would be the Law of Karma.

form of change or movement. This interaction is a universal law where nothing is allowed to remain static.

The Christian doctrine is based upon the Trinity of the Father, Son and Holy Ghost. The three united to create our universe. In physics, the combination of two atoms of hydrogen with one oxygen produces water. One early twentieth century esoteric school of philosophy based its beliefs on the concept that the universe required the trinity of an active, passive and neutralizing force to create mental progression. In numerology, three is a number of completion, the beginning, middle and end. And, this Law of Three is perfectly represented within the geometric structure of quartz.

Structure

In geological terms, crystals are classified as minerals. However, not all minerals are crystals—only those with a regular atomic structure forming a crystalline pattern. There are six (some references state seven with the trigonal separate from the hexagonal) basic patterns called the isometric, tetragonal, hexagonal or trigonal, orthorhombic, monoclinic, and triclinic. Quartz, classified under the hexagonal category, forms a tetrahedron, an equilateral triangle with three sides, a base and all angles each measuring 60 degrees. The tetrahedron repeats itself by duplicating an open left or right spiral within the body of the crystal. The right or clockwise spiral is believed to be indigenous to those crystals found north of the equator, while the left counterclock-

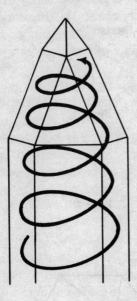 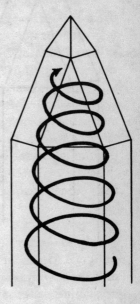

Left   **Right**

LEFT AND RIGHT SPIRAL

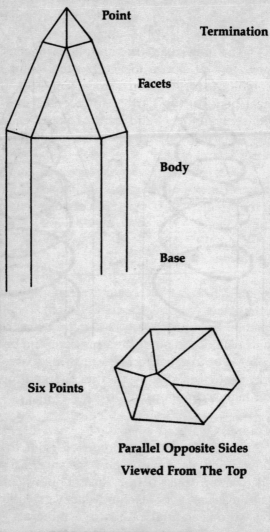

Point

Termination

Facets

Body

Base

Six Points

Parallel Opposite Sides

Viewed From The Top

PARTS OF A CRYSTAL

wise twist is found in crystals south of the equator. The direction of the spiral in no way affects the energy properties of the quartz.

The molecular structure of quartz consists of one atom of silicon to two oxygen atoms which combine to form silicon dioxide. Compression and heat beneath the Earth's surface coalesce these molecules into the solid shape of quartz. Each point has six facets, and each opposite side of the body is always parallel.

Quartz symbolizes perfection with the universal structure of the triangle spiraling to completion. It represents Nature's creation of a beginning, middle and end.

Inclusions

Quartz, along with other minerals, grows beneath the Earth's surface, most commonly in beds of igneous (volcanic) rock. This crystal will often contain impurities from minerals such as copper, tourmaline, and other semi-precious and precious stones due to a sharing of the growing space. These inclusions will slightly alter its energy properties for higher consciousness work.

Colored Quartz

Color in quartz is produced from traces of other minerals. Amethyst, for instance, is a purple shade due to traces of iron. Rose or pink quartz contains manganese or titanium. Smoky gray is formed by various natural radioactive minerals. These microscopic-sized additions alter the properties of the quartz which in turn subtly affect the characteristics of the released electromagnetic energy.

All quartz initially grows with six facets. These facets refer to the flat portion of the body which joins together to form a termination, the culmination of which is a point or apex.

Colorless Quartz

References made to quartz crystal in this book will concern the clear, colorless varieties without mineral traces or inclusions unless otherwise stated. The clear color gives quartz the capacity to absorb and reflect all color vibrations within the spectrum of light. This makes it a unique healing instrument which brings light and energy into our physical and spiritual bodies.

The termination is most often colorless, while its body is usually a milky white color. This murky portion is trapped water vapor and does not detract from the crystal's energies. Absolutely clear, unclouded quartz is difficult to obtain.

Crystals vary in size from less than one inch to several feet in height and diameter. Quartz sold in mineral shops tends to be less than four inches. The larger ones ranging from up to four feet are rare, expensive and very difficult to come by. When purchasing crystals, size should not be an important factor in the beginning stages of working with their energies.

Shapes

The most common mining areas for quartz in

the Western Hemisphere are Brazil in South America, and Arkansas in the United States. Depending on the growing space and mining procedures, these stones are available for sale in clusters, single points double terminated points, and chunks.

Clusters

Clusters are the most common grouping of quartz points. They grow naturally in close proximity to one another and share a common base. There may be as few as two or as many as hundreds living in this arrangement. Each individual within the family of a cluster has its own unique energy pattern, yet all are in harmony with one another. This relationship can be compared to a number of musical instruments in an orchestra. When played separately, each has a distinctive sound, but when played in unison they blend to form a single composite harmony.

The energy is emitted in a sporadic manner with the single points constantly recharging one another. As well as their use in a meditative and healing capacity, the cluster's recharging process can be used to purify the air. "For example, if an argument has taken place in a certain room, quartz clusters could be placed in that area to purify the environment of negative energies and feelings."[2]

The crystals found growing in clusters usually have single points. Occasionally there may be double terminations or a combination of both singles and doubles.

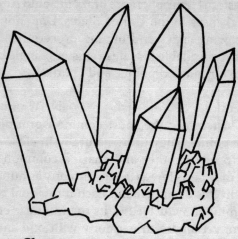

Cluster

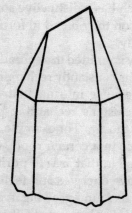

Single Point

CRYSTAL TYPES

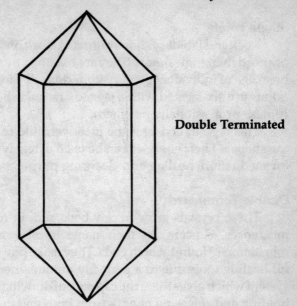

Double Terminated

Chunk

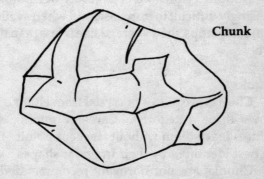

CRYSTAL TYPES

Single Points

Rock and lapidary shops normally stock plenty of affordable single points. They are obtained by the breakage of individual points within clusters. Single points are six-faceted with a jagged, irregular base (unless professionally polished).

This type of crystal is the most versatile of all the shapes. Their energies can be used extensively for meditation, healing and cleansing purposes.

Double Terminated

These crystals grow in clay beds and, in rare incidences, clusters. As their name implies, terminations are found at both ends. They make powerful healing tools due to a perfectly unique energy system which gives them the capacity of drawing in, holding and releasing energy from both ends.

Double terminated crystals are becoming increasingly difficult to purchase, and when available from rock shops, their average size is less than three inches.

Chunks

Chunks are pieces of crystal from either of the above three categories. Careless mining procedures leave them without facets or points. They are best identified by their irregular shapes.

Chunks are not normally recommended for use in healing configurations because they are missing the necessary points for energy linking. They do, however, make excellent tools for focusing the mind in meditation. These pieces can also be placed in water containers to energize and purify tap water. (Refer to Chapter 11 for further details.)

Polished Quartz

Various crystal users dispute whether or not polished quartz (cut and faceted by machines) contains more energy than the natural stone. Uncut quartz has an advantage in that the vibrations have not been disturbed by mankind. To some people, this means the crystal is in its pure form as a virtually untouched product from nature. This variety is less expensive to purchase, can be personally mined, and is more accessible than polished crystal.

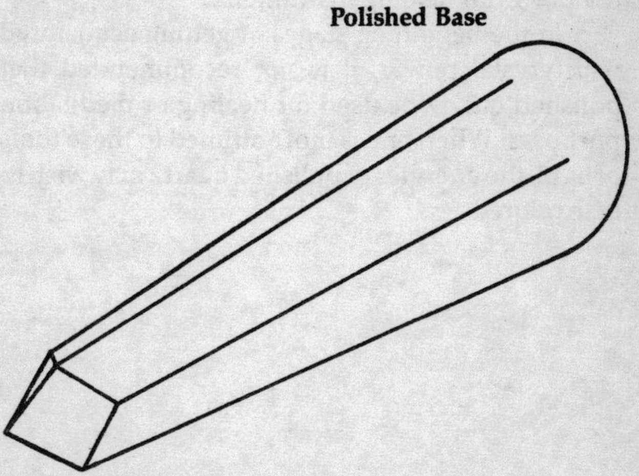

Polished Base

Laser Beam Point

POLISHED QUARTZ

Polished quartz does have some benefits. It is aesthetically pleasing with all facets and the point intact. The milkiness found in natural quartz is missing, the base is smooth, and it can be shaped with more than six facets. Marcel Vogel, a noted crystal worker, discovered that by cutting and faceting the crystal's storage capacity was increased. This made it a more directed tool for performing extensive etheric healings and mind thought projections.

A type of polished quartz depicted in the diagram on page 17 has a sharp point that produces almost a laser beam of amplified energy. Such a stone with the curved base and perfect point makes it a powerful healing instrument.

In the beginning stages of getting acquainted with crystal power, it is not recommended that polished quartz be used for healing or meditation purposes. When one is more attuned to these tools of light, the energies of polished quartz may wish to be explored.

3

ENERGY FIELDS

Vibrations surround all matter. Sound, color, light, minerals, humans, etc., all vibrate at varying frequencies but still have the ability to interact with one another. When the energies of quartz are added to our own, a newly combined vibrational force is created. This interaction can best be compared to the rippling action of simultaneously throwing two stones into a still pond. When they break the water's surface, two separate series of waves are produced. A precise blending takes place as each concentric ring spreads out and begins to intermingle with the other. Crystals are like one stone, we are like the other. When placed together, our vibrations will merge in perfect harmony to help us raise our energies into higher levels of awareness.

Crystal Energy Fields

Quartz crystals are natural conductors of electromagnetic energy. Each moving electron produces an energy field. A regular, even flow of electromagnetic energy moves freely through the crystal's structure. This freedom of movement is made possible by the molecular structure of spiraling equilateral triangles. Energy is drawn into and through the body of the crystal and then projected out its termination(s). The energy that is released can be stimulated by body heat, direct sunlight, contact with other crystals, various metals or programmed mind thoughts. Any of these interactions will excite the electrons into transforming energy.

The emitted energy can be compared to the vibrations produced by a group of people with a unanimous thought; the difference is that the crystal energy is uniformly constant. This consistent effect makes them the best tools for creating a harmonious balance between our physical and spiritual selves. They will help to realign any imbalanced energies and remove blockages which can prevent new levels of awareness from filtering into the conscious mind.

Crystals can become an extension of our own vibrations. Their energy will intermingle with our own, and when properly programmed, can liberate the mind into discovering potentially unlimited awareness.

Human Energy Fields

We operate on a similar principle of electromagnetism. When our hands touch an object, electrical impulses move through our body. Vibrations are sent through the fingers along the body's

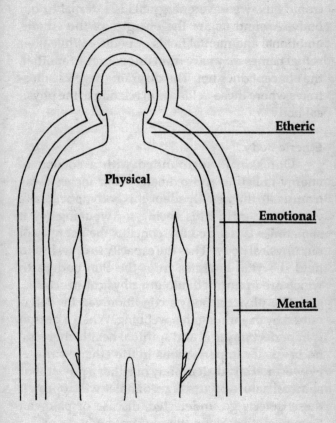

THE BODIES

nervous system for the object's identity to be interpreted by our brain. Along with this internal electronic flux, we have energy fields external to our body. Around us are the energies of the etheric, emotional and mental fields or bodies. While their actual names may vary from one source to another, the concept does not. The diagram (page 21) illustrates where these fields are in relation to the physical body.

Etheric Body

Our skin is surrounded with a cocoon of energy radiating approximately four inches away from us. To the visually adept, this body appears as a violet-gray mist. This casing, or webbing (as it sometimes is referred to), contains the energies of our physical body. It has the capacity to draw in and hold the vital energies from the Sun and Earth which are in turn fed into our physical structure.

The physical body's condition can be determined by examining this webbing. When a person is in perfect physical and spiritual health, there are no breaks or imperfections in the etheric surface. However, if any disharmony of either a physical or spiritual nature occurs, tears or holes will appear. If these defects go undetected, disease or pain can become noticeable in the physical body.

Spiritual Bodies

Around the etheric, often extending for several feet, flows the energies of the emotional and mental bodies. These two vibrational fields are called the spiritual bodies.

The emotional portion (also called the astral) stores such feelings as fear, courage, joy, sorrow, love and hate. Liberated emotions are subsequently released to the physical structure by individual triggers. For example, the death of a close friend may elicit the response of sorrow. The more intense this feeling, the more messages will be relayed from the emotional body to its physical counterpart. A corresponding response may be crying, shaking or sickness.

The mental component of the spiritual bodies can be described as ". . . the essence of active intelligence. It has qualities such as: rules, regulations, evaluation, discipline, control and judgement."[1] Like the emotional body, any disharmony may result in physical symptoms. For example, if a person commits an immoral act (meaning the act goes against his or her internal belief system), that person may then unconsciously punish the physical self with disease.

The mental body acts as a balance between the etheric and emotional aspects by utilizing ". . . active intelligence, discipline, memory, judgement and discrimination to evaluate and process the data."[2] It decides what will and will not filter into the other bodies.

A chain reaction can occur when the emotional and mental portions of the spiritual bodies direct the etheric which in turn affects the conditions of the physical structure. In order for us to be in perfect holistic health, a balance between all bodies needs to be first achieved and then maintained.

Aura

A combination of the etheric and spiritual bodies results in what is known as the human aura. Webster's dictionary describes this energy field as "an air, a subtle influence or quality emanating from or surrounding a person or object." Kirlian photography is said to demonstrate this electromagnetic field surrounding humans, plants, animals and other matter with a coronal image.

The soul is believed to be contained within this aura. It is both an ancient and universal opinion that this fom survives man after death. This soul radiates the color vibrations of the three bodies. For those with developed spiritual sight, the clarity of colors emitted is an indication of conditions within the spiritual and physical bodies. As well as health, it is believed that observations can be made concerning the person's past lives, future events and spiritual guides.

A distinction should be made at this time for the reader so that he/she can understand the difference between what is called psychic and spiritual. The psychic world refers to those aspects that relate to what is commonly known as the fourth dimension. Mediums, psychics, and seers can reach through the veil that blocks most people from seeing more than what's apparent in the third dimension. From the fourth dimension they can receive information about past lives and possible upcoming situations, and speak to spirits. The spiritual realms are thought to be the fifth and sixth dimension relating to pure energy or intelligence forms (sometimes called our masters and teachers). Some refer to this as higher consciousness, or being in touch with the soul. When people develop their conscious awareness to a high degree, they then have entered into a level of spirituality or union with their higher self. They do not become "psychics," but rather follow that silent, inner, intuitive voice which directs them in their daily activities.

Crystal and Human Energies

In order to gain more conscious knowledge about our emotional, intellectual and physical states, we share our energies with crystals. The coupling of our relatively inconsistent vibrations with the balancing ones of quartz can bridge the gap between our physical, etheric and spiritual selves. This is achieved through the use of crystal meditations and healings.

4

DEVELOPMENT INSTRUMENTS

It is believed that the necessary types of crystals will arrive to assist each seeker genuinely searching for inner awakening. These instruments for development may materialize as gifts, or be purchased in the form of personal, generator and/or healing crystals.

Personal Crystals

A personal crystal with programming will become the most important tool to unlock hidden areas within your mind. When its vibrations have become totally integrated with those of your own, a harmonious relationship will begin. This quartz can amplify inner growth when you are in a meditative, sleeping or waking state. It will become an extension of your conscious and yet unexplored self.

Special care should be taken when selecting this instrument for development. Try and obtain a single point with an intact point and all six facets visible on its surface. If the point is chipped, the energy emitted will not be as focused. It should also be small enough to hold in one hand. The suggested sizes can range from less than two inches to five inches in height and diameter. If you are right-hand dominate, the quartz's vibrations can be tested by holding the crystal point up toward the head in your left hand. The point is placed up rather than down in order to direct the energies into your brain. The left hand is preferred as it is connected to the opposite side of the brain. This is the right hemisphere, the intuitive portion of our mind. For those people who are left-hand dominate, the holding process should be reversed.

After holding the stone for a few minutes, some people may experience energy vibrations in the form of body temperature changes, colors flashing through the mind, or a feeling of peaceful compatibility. If any uncomfortable sensations are experienced, choose another crystal and repeat the same process. It is imperative for you to feel synchronized with its energies.

Often a stone will choose *us* by projecting strong vibrations. It is not uncommon to walk away from such a crystal only to discover a compulsion to return and purchase it.

The most aesthetically pleasing is not necessarily the correct crystal. If the vibrations are compatible, do not be concerned if it has a milky base. This cloudy crystal can be considered a reflection of your own development. The yet untapped subconscious is symbolically the quartz's misty portion, while the conscious self is like its clear apex. You must strive to bring the subconscious, hidden, intuitive aspects of your mind up to the conscious level in order for you to become a perfectly clear crystal. As this inner awareness starts taking place, the crystal often begins to clear. This cloudy area may be considered as a personal mirror reflecting your progress.

After cleansing (see Chapter 5 for complete cleansing instructions), a new crystal should be carried on or near the body as it needs time to absorb, blend with and become an extension of your personal vibrations. Keep it close by when performing such daily routines as working, reading and relaxing. It should even be slept with by tucking the quartz between the bottom pillow case and the bed. Be sure that the point is directed up away from your head for higher spiritual awareness.

It is well researched that the majority of people are able to recall only those dreams which the subconscious chooses to release to the conscious mind. Using a personal crystal can cause an increase in dream guidance and recall. If you have an urgent problem that needs to be solved by the next day, hold the stone in both hands point up and request that a solution be received through dream guidance. The problem may work itself out in the dream state. To recall the solution, hold the crystal once again upon awakening.

In order for this personal crystal to become an effective development tool, thirty days should be allowed for a total vibrational integration to take place.

If it is too large or cumbersome for carrying close to the body, a second smaller one is recommended. This one can be worn as jewelry or placed in a pocket or purse. If carried, it should be wrapped in a soft natural cloth to protect the easily chipped point. Never place any crystal in plastic wrappings or manmade materials, as its effectiveness will be reduced. Your personal vibrations will be blocked from intermingling with those of the crystal's.

Crystals may be worn as jewelry in the form of rings, necklaces, bracelets or earrings, or secured under watch bands. The most effective wearing method is in a pendant style with the crystal falling in the center of the chest. For those people who wish to be more grounded to the physical, everyday world, a *single point* pendant is recommended with the point directed toward the feet. If a spiritual uplifting is needed, the termination should be positioned up toward the head. A *double terminated* neck piece will create a perfectly balanced effect between the physical and higher vibrations.

Some suggested metals to use for mounting crystal jewelry pieces are copper, silver or gold. Copper is the best conductor of body energy. "It has the ability of drawing off things which are within the body; the ability of drawing off the dregs of many things from the body, by oxidizing through the pores and eliminating some of the metallic wastes within."[1] The crystal will amplify this effect. When properly programmed, this wearing arrangement can be powerful for cleansing and energizing the body.

It is thought that a smaller quartz will attune itself to the wearer's vibrations in a shorter length of time than the larger personal size. This process is usually completed within fifteen days because it is in constant contact with the skin. When in harmonious vibrations with its owner, the crystal will act as an energizer for the physical, etheric and spiritual bodies. Further details on crystal jewelry are given in Chapter 10.

Generators

Generators are usually the largest quartz in a person's collection. They can be used as the power source to activate other crystals for linking in healing and meditation layouts.

When crystals are not in use, place them in a circular pattern around the generator for recharging. This arrangement will provide a constant energy flow, and keep them fully energized.

Large generators, over one foot in height, can be used as a focal point for projecting thoughts. They are often used as such in meditation groups. The people sit in a circle around this powerful crystal and energize it through mental thoughts.

Healing Crystals

These are multi-purpose tools to be used in healing and meditation configurations. Healing crystals, when programmed, will serve as amplifiers

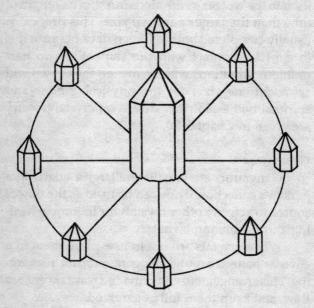

GENERATOR ENERGIZING CRYSTALS

of the healer's and/or meditator's own body energy. They will also balance and realign any inharmonious vibrations when placed around a person in a healing layout (refer to Chapter 7 for more details).

These can be of various sizes and shapes. It is not important if they are chipped or cracked; only the points need to be intact.

Suggestions

A crystal may not appear to have any obvious use in a healing, personal or generating capacity. There are many such stones whose powers have not yet been activated by a compatible mind. If you were to purchase one of these or received it as a gift, place it aside until your inner awareness becomes more developed. Your intuition will then direct you to this special crystal's function.

An owner may outgrow the energies of a particular quartz. It can cease to be of any further assistance as a development tool. When this occurs, give it to someone who can utilize the vibrations.

It is recommended that each new quartz be examined in detail. Take the time to hold it; become familiar with its texture, weight and temperature. Look for any unusual markings on its body. Inspect the internal structure. Watch how sunlight reflects the colors of the spectrum through it. Check periodically for structural changes and clearing. In other words, get to know your crystal as you would a new house or automobile. As is done with plants, some people talk and play music to their crystals. They become "friends." Do what comes naturally from the intuitive rather than from the logical center of your mind.

Last but not least, enjoy these instruments for your development.

5

CRYSTAL CARE

In order to properly serve an awakening mind, crystals, like all delicate instruments, require special care and treatment. Eventually each crystal worker will intuitively develop his/her own caring techniques. In the interim, this chapter offers some basic guidelines to help get you started.

Soaking/Cleansing

Cleansing should always be performed immediately after acquiring or purchasing a crystal, because many people will have handled it. Their vibrations will be retained upon its surface. Always assume these are negative, noncompatible energies which shouldn't intermingle with your own.

A virgin quartz, one that has been recently mined, has also been handled during the mining and shipping process. A cleansing will help to soothe and balance the jostled electromagnetic fields before work is begun with its energies.

It should be a personal decision whether or not to cleanse a crystal that has been received as a gift. The giver's vibrations may or not be congenial with yours.

Sea salt is the recommended cleanser to remove and purify surface vibrations. It neutralizes the quartz's electrical surface charges while not affecting the embedded program. Soaking solution is made with one cup of sea salt in its crystalline form to one quart of water. Ideally, the water should not be any warmer than the temperature of the crystal. The way of checking for this is to hold the stone in one hand while running tap water over the other until a compatible water temperature is reached. *Never* use a metallic container to hold this solution. The sensitive electrons in the quartz can become damaged by the magnetic field set up between the salt and the container. Before immersing the crystal, hold it in the left hand (both hands if it is a large size) and mentally request that all negativity be removed.

Many experienced crystal workers tune in to the immersed stone and intuitively know when it has been cleansed. The beginner should allow the soaking time to range from 15 minutes to several hours depending on where the quartz was obtained. Those from a crystal shop need at least twenty-four hours to ensure that all accumulated vibrations have been removed. When the cleansing is complete, the quartz is washed under cool, running water to activate its energy flow. A soft brush may be used to remove any debris. The last step is to rub it with a natural fabric such as cotton or silk. The stone is now ready for programming.

Programming

Crystals are portable computers with the capability of receiving, storing and releasing upon command. Even its programming is similar to that of a computer's. Both require clear, logical input to extract concise output. The difference between the two methods of information input is that the computer programmer needs complicated machine language while the crystal worker uses simple, everyday pictorial thoughts. The following steps will demonstrate to the reader how this is done.

STEP 1: CLEARING

Before embedding a program, the quartz must be cleared of any previous thoughts. It should be held point up in the left hand. If it is too large for this, place the crystal point up on a flat surface. With the left hand touching or covering the base, mentally direct an imaginary beam of white light to flow through this hand into the base, up through the body and out the point.

This light should then be passed through the sides until it is intuitively felt that the quartz has been cleared of any previous programming. Always use the color white for clearing as it is the purest form of vibrational energy, representing the sum total of all colors. When cleared, the crystal is like a blank tape ready for recording.

STEP 2: FORMULATING A PROGRAM

In the beginning stages, it is recommended to limit one program per crystal. If more than one is used, the separate programs may create an output of confused and conflicting messages which can contradict one another. Keep the program as simple as possible, leaving more complicated projections for a later date.

Each quartz should be programmed with its owner's best interests in mind. This means formulating a thought that includes images of self-growth and development. Care must be taken that no negative impressions are to be embedded within any crystal, for such a program would be magnified and reflected back. All instilled images will be amplified within the quartz's spiraling triangles, released and then manifested.

Crystals do not respond to verbal language, so each program needs to be carefully thought out in sequential picture form. Sounds and colors can be instilled for higher levels of programming, but for the beginner, visualized pictorial events are recommended. Some suggestions for this type of programming are given below.

Personal Crystals

Crystals to be either worn, used in meditation or for personal development may be programmed with self-images. This is accomplished by mentally picturing yourself in perfect health and happiness. In other words, see yourself as you wish to be. When projecting this image into the crystal, it is advisable to surround your body with a protective shield to repel any type of negativity from entering into your auric field. This is done by creating an imaginary bubble around your entire physical structure. Its size may be six inches to three feet, whatever is most comfortable. Create this protective coating so that you may see out and experience the world, but no negative emotions or situations may enter into your vibrations. Some people construct a mirror around the outside of their shield reflecting back any negativity to the external source. It is a personal choice. Do whatever you feel is right for you.

Another suggested program is one for increased awareness. A self-image may be projected with a pure, white light surrounding the body aura. This will attract the higher vibrations from the universal frequencies to hasten your development process. You are, in effect, placing your physical and spiritual bodies in the hands of the so-called higher forces that be. Depending upon your belief system, this may be your soul, your god, your guides or whatever you wish to call these forces.

If a crystal worker desires to be a better healer, channeler of information, artist, etc., a projected picture of this completed goal can be instilled. For example, if one wishes to do crystal healings, this person should visualize him/herself actually performing a successful treatment.

There is no end to the possibilities for self-growth. The programmer should always be realistic and completely certain about what is desired, for it will be received. It may not be exactly what is expected, nor may the request come immediately, but be assured, it *will* manifest. Keep in the mind the old saying, "Be careful what you ask for, you may just get it!"

Healing Crystals

Healing crystals may be programmed for the removal of spiritual and physical ailments. Each crystal may be implanted with a mental picture of a treated person in perfect health. If there is a specific problem to be alleviated, program by visualizing the disease dissipating in a "cloud of smoke," or see that person in a perfect state of health.

Gift Crystals

When a crystal is programmed for a gift, the recipient should be pictured inside its structure in perfect health and harmony with life. This quartz may be carried or worn directly on the giver's body for a number of days to imprint his/her vibrations. These will eventually become intermingled with those of the new owner's.

Gift crystals can be programmed to remove development blockages, assist in healing, help in meditation, or anything the receiver needs assistance with. Always tell this person what the program is and let it be his/her decision whether or not it is compatible with his/her vibrations and/or development.

Generator Crystals

These may be programmed as a linking force to activate and recharge other crystals by visualizing a beam of white light. Some people program large generators with projections for world peace by picturing all races and countries in perfect peace and harmony.

If you have a specific material need such as a car, house, job or whatever is lacking in your life (keeping in mind that it must be in your highest interests), a picture of this may be placed under the base. The thought form when combined with the mechanical picture increases the strength of the program.

STEP 3: INSTILLING THE PROGRAM

Each crystal type requires a slight variation when instilling a program.

Single Points

Small crystals may be held with the left hand covering the base while the right is cupped over the point. Larger sizes may be placed "point up" on a flat surface. If the base is too irregular to rest safely on a surface, mold some plasticine or material around it. The left hand should be touching as near its base as possible, and the right cupping the point (see the following diagram).

The program may now be instilled. The thought form will run from your mind to the hand holding the crystal base, run up through its body to the point and flow back into the programmer to complete the

Small Single Point

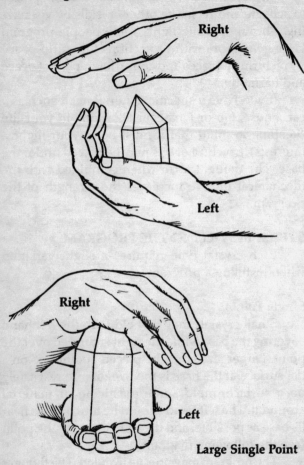

Right

Left

Right

Left

Large Single Point

PROGRAMMING CRYSTALS

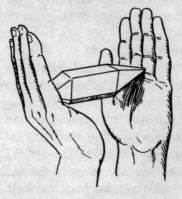

Double Terminated Quartz

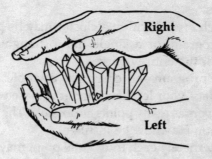

Quartz Cluster

PROGRAMMING CRYSTALS

circuit. The heat from your hands will excite the electrons within the crystal's structure to cause increased energy to surge through its point.

Double Terminated Quartz

Hold double terminated quartz between the palms of your hands with the two ends bridging the centers as if in prayer. Project the program. The thought will run in a circuit from the mind into each point simultaneously. The electrons in each termination will flow toward the center of the crystal where they become intermingled and radiate out to the opposite point running back and forth, amplifying and magnifying the thought. Since there are two terminations, the program will be very powerful.

Clusters

Each crystal within a cluster may be given its own program, or a single mind thought can be made for the entire quartz.

To program the cluster as a whole thought form, place your left hand under its base while the right covers as many points as possible. The thought projection may now be instilled

Alternately each individual point may be programmed by placing the palm of the right hand over each individual point and projecting the thought form while the left holds its base. All programs should be of compatible nature since the energies share a common base.

Program Repetition

To ensure that a program has been sufficiently embedded, the same images should be projected repeatedly into the crystal for a period of seven days. Depending upon the complexity of the program, once a day for a few minutes is usually all the time that is required.

Through this repetition, both the mind and crystal become conditioned to accept and receive the program. The mind psychologically begins to set up the conditions for the desired response while the crystal repeatedly amplifies the thought.

Negativity

There may be a rare occasion when, after soaking, clearing and programming, negativity can still be detected in a crystal. Negativity can best be described as an incompatibility with its owner's vibrations. A burning feeling may be experienced while holding it, unpleasant images may be projected out of this crystal in meditation, or it may intuitively not "feel" right. With negative programming so deeply instilled, this crystal will never be a development tool. The best solution is to bury it in a remote location and forget its existence.

General Cleansing

Quartz should be rinsed under cool tap water every two weeks. This washing will remove any surface build-up of dust, which can reduce its effectiveness. The stone may then be rubbed with a soft natural fiber to further stimulate its energy fields.

Healing crystals absorb the vibrations from emotional and physical ailments during a treatment. To prevent these energies from contaminating other crystals as well as people, soak them in a salt solution for no less than fifteen minutes. The length of cleansing may be judged by the degree of the person's emotional reaction when in the crystal arrangement. Crying, sobbing, shaking etc., indicates a large amount of negativity was removed. In such a case, play it safe and increase the soaking time to twenty-four hours.

It should be emphasized that it is possible for the healer to absorb the recipient's negativity into his/her body aura. To prevent possible emotional contamination or physical reactions from occurring, the healer should wash both hands under running water after each session. This will remove the negative vibrations from the body. Whenever possible, a complete body shower is recommended.

If crystals are being washed in a stream, lake or ocean, make sure they are tightly held (in both hands). They have a tendency to leap away from the washer to return to their natural origins, and are next to impossible to see underwater.

Energizing

Crystals need natural light and should be given a minimum of five hours per week in direct sunlight for energizing. Place them on sunny window sills, balconies or in safe spots out of doors.

They will also charge/energize by being kept

in close proximity to one another. It is suggested that their energy be allowed to flow by placing the crystals in a triangular or circular shape.

Smaller ones are best recharged by placing them on or in between the points of a cluster.

Precautions

To prevent damage to crystals some suggested precautions are:

- do not expose them to long periods of artificial light, particularly fluorescent. Their molecular structure can become altered and permanently damaged by the bending effects of unnatural light frequencies.

- do not place crystals on magnetic surfaces. The programs can be erased by repolarization.

- do not reuse a salt solution after cleansing. The salt holds the old vibrations and will release these back into the new crystals.

- do not touch other people's crystals unless invited to do so. They may not wish your vibrations to be incorporated into their quartz.

- do not allow anyone to handle your personal crystal. The vibrations have been specifically tuned to your own.

- do not go near your crystals when in a deressed or angry state. They will pick up on your negativity, amplify and release it back to you.

When transporting crystals, wrap each one separately in a soft, natural material. Ensure that the points are well protected.

6

POSSIBLE SIDE EFFECTS

Crystals are powerful tools. Some discomfort may be experienced when working with their energies. The reader should become familiar with possible side effects before using crystals on others or on oneself. Tolerance to these new energies must be built up slowly.

Headaches

During a healing or meditation, pain in the form of a headache may be felt most intensely in the center of the forehead. This reaction is created from the energy fields of the crystal modulating with those of the brain. This energy can flow through the center of the forehead where it is believed to affect the pineal gland, called the third eye. (This center will be fully discussed in Chapter 7.) These headaches should be considered as part of the positive process of stimulating the intuitive centers of the mind.

If headaches occur during a healing or meditation, the crystals should be removed. The discomfort may last anywhere from a few minutes to a day, depending on how much that person is sensitized or overcharged. Too much energy has filtered into the body too quickly. Each of us has an individual tolerance which can only be found through cautious experimentation.

Energy Tingles

These tiny, almost electrical shocks similar to dull needles are often felt on different parts of the body during crystal work. Under normal conditions, they only last for a few minutes. However, after an intensive healing, it is not uncommon to experience them for up to forty-eight hours. They usually affect areas of the body that have suffered damage to the etheric webbing and are evidence of the crystal energies remaining at work trying to smooth over these imperfections.

Along with tingles, the body's temperature may alternate between hot and cold. The heat is due to a pulling in of the crystal energies, while the cold is a giving-off of excess energy in order to maintain a balance.

Should any of these sensations become too intense to handle during healing or meditation, remove the crystals. Work slowly, allowing the body to build up tolerance to the power. This is a process that cannot be rushed.

Numbness

The hands and forearms may experience a numbing effect, particularly when using a crystal to charge layouts. This reaction is caused by the electromagnetic flux flowing between the crystals and the person experiencing this charge. The feeling will promptly be alleviated by removing the quartz.

Diarrhea/Upset Stomach

Overexposure to quartz energy may cause diarrhea and/or queasiness. If either symptom develops, the power of the crystal is too much for the person to handle at that time.

If either reaction occurs while the person is wearing a new crystal, it should be downsized to a smaller, less powerful one. If it is a double-terminated quartz, exchange it for a single point. The physical body's internal organs are not yet adjusted to these new energies. Slowly increase the wearing time until the body is not affected.

If copper wire is wrapped around it, a substitution for a less conductive metal such as gold or silver will usually alleviate the problem.

Should the symptoms still persist, cut down the wearing time to two hours a day until the body's tolerance has been increased. Then gradually begin to lengthen the time.

If a healing arrangement is thought to be the cause of diarrhea or an upset stomach, let the person receiving the treatment fully recover before the sessions are resumed. A week will usually allow full release of the physical and/or spiritual blockages.

Negativity

When people first start to work with crystal energies, it is quite possible for them to experience some negative emotional reactions. As soon as conscious development begins, we all become increasingly sensitive to all external situations. We are more "finely tuned" like a radio receiver and so are susceptible to vibrations. What may never have bothered us before suddenly becomes very upsetting. This must be accepted as part of the awareness process. There are no simple ways of dealing with it. Just understand and put up with it knowing it is an indication of progression.

Lightheadedness

The sensation of being lightheaded or dizzy often occurs after an intensive healing. This is an indication that emotional burdens have been released. It is possible to feel in a different space or to have a sense of severing with reality. This altered state passes quickly.

Exceptions

Some people will never experience any of these problems. Be assured that reactions can and are occurring both to the physical and spiritual self without necessarily having any overt symptoms.

If sensations appear to stop after extended work with crystal energies, this should be taken as a positive indication that the body has adjusted to the energies. Such individuals are now capable of working with more powerful crystal arrangements.

7

CRYSTAL MEDITATIONS

By means of Meditation man learns to concentrate and project his attention straight through the physical plane to the Fourth Dimension, then later to further dimensions. He endeavors to bring that which he learns through into the physical world, translated into physical language and interpreted into his own brain as best he can. . . He is getting into the heart of things, the underlying causes, the primordial truths.[1]

Access to the silent inner self is achieved through the art of meditation. The word "meditation" is derived from the Greek word *medonai* which translated means 'to think about it.' "Art" is an acquired skill. It is absolutely imperative that this "skill of thinking" be developed by everyone who is seeking to unblock the intuitive energies of their minds. Without it, little personal growth or development will come about.

Meditation shuts down the conscious thought patterns allowing the subconscious or inner self to flow freely, relieved of censorship. This process induces an altered state of awareness. Crystals should be considered as the intermediary instruments of choice for enhancing this opening of the mind. When combined with proper meditation techniques, progress is literally a thought away.

Set aside a fixed time each day for meditation. Like sleeping, waking and eating, it will eventually be incorporated into the body's biological clock system and become more effective.

Before starting into the mechanics of the following exercises, the reader should become familiar with the role that colors play in meditation.

We can all identify with the value they have in stimulating our emotions. Psychologists have shown that the color red will invoke anger, blue elicits peace, yellow is stimulating to the intellect, orange promotes self-confidence, and so on. Men and women pay to have their colors done by experts who match skin tones to flattering colors. Interior designers coordinate color schemes to enhance a room. This color awareness is all around us, but utilized mainly at a subconscious level. For meditation purposes, these color vibrations will be used at a conscious level.

Each color within our three-dimensional world has its own unique qualities. For example, red has properties of inducing strength and power to a person who is suffering from a lack of energy. Indigo (purplish blue) will produce increased awareness to overcome spiritual blockages. The properties of these colors and their uses are shown in the following table.

COLORS AND THEIR QUALITIES

COLOR	PROPERTIES	WHEN TO USE
Red	strength, power	lack of vitality, depression
Orange	self-confidence, courage	insecurity, self-doubts
Yellow	happiness, stimulation	fear, stress, tension
Green	healing, balance	selfishness, jealousy
Blue	peace, serenity	nervousness, restlessness
Indigo	intuition, awareness	lack of decisiveness, blockages
Violet	creativity, enlightenment	boredom, lack of spiritual growth
White	purity, encompassing all colors	completion, protection

Before meditating, decide what condition needs to be altered, and then select the appropriate color that will assist and complement.

CRYSTAL MEDITATION #1
THE PYRAMID

For the beginner, the choice of a place for meditation needs to be carefully selected. Someone more experienced will be able to drift into this altered state regardless of the surroundings. Choose an area that is both quiet and dimly lit. Sometimes soft, tranquil music is helpful for focusing the mind and blocking any distracting noises. Various meditation tapes are available with music and voice-induction techniques. Mandalas can also be used to quiet the left brain with endless geometric mazes. Or, mind/will power can be used. The idea is to shut off the left, mechanical portion of the mind while allowing a free flowing of the right, intuitive center.

Sit either on the floor or in a straight-backed chair. All restrictive clothing should be loosened. The objective is to make oneself as comfortable as possible without falling asleep.

Read through this first exercise, then sit with both feet flat on the floor or use the lotus position. The personal crystal can be held either in the left or both hands, resting on the lap.

Step One

- Close the eyes.

- Take three consecutive short breaths in through the nose, filling up the lungs.

- Hold each breath for the count of three.

- Breathe out from the mouth with pursed lips in three short breaths, expelling all the air from your lungs.

- Repeat this process two more times. A slight lightheadedness may be experienced. Do not overdo it.

Step Two

- Count backwards from 9 to 1 to set up a deep, natural, rhythmic breathing pattern.

- Mentally inform your biological timer to bring you back to full conscious awareness in fifteen minutes. If you do not trust this internal clock, have someone interrupt the session at the end of the predetermined time. It is surprising, though, how accurate your bio-timer becomes with practice.

Step Three

- With eyes still shut, choose a color to work with what best suits your present emotional condition.

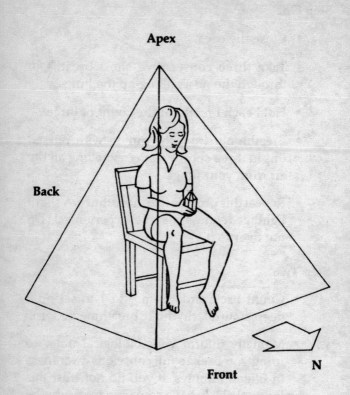

Apex

Back

Front

N

Sitting in a Chair

THE PYRAMID

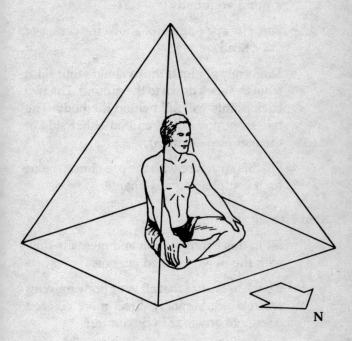

Lotus Position

THE PYRAMID

Step Four

- Mentally construct a four-sided pyramid around your body.

- Form its apex one foot above the center of your head.

- Uniformly graduate the pyramid's four sides from the apex down to the ground. The two back points will fall behind the body. The two front points will end on either side of the feet (see diagram).

- Fill this structure with the pre-chosen color for a complete energy charge.

Step Five

- Sit in this configuration and mentally flow with the newly created energies.

- Check to ensure that all your body muscles are relaxed. Mentally direct more colored energy to any area in discomfort.

- Try and allow all thoughts within your mind to flow freely. Eventually the conscious chatter will cease as an altered state of awareness is allowed to drift in. It may take several sittings before this fully occurs.

Step Six

- When the preset 15 minutes have elapsed, slowly count up from 1 to 9.

- Open your eyes and become aware of your body and the crystal.

- Mentally erase the pyramid structure.

Reflections

The imaginary pyramid structure is the space which will hold the energies of the personal crystal and any thought projections from the mind. In this beginning stage, the concept of the structure is all the meditator needs to be concerned about. With practice, the mind will become conditioned to project thought forms outside the body.

This meditation may be repeated the same time each day for at least one week or until the meditator feels completely at ease with the energies.

CRYSTAL MEDITATION #2
ADVANCED PYRAMID STRUCTURE

This second exercise is designed to take the meditator a step closer to working with both crystal and body energies. If any spiritual or physical discomfort is experienced, stop the session at once. Return to the first meditation until both the mind and body are capable of tolerating more powerful energy vibrations.

Step One

- Follow the same procedure as in Meditation One of sitting and holding the crystal.

- Relax the mind and body with the same breathing techniques.

- Set your mental timer for 15 minutes.

Step Two

- Create the pyramid structure using the blue color for understanding, acceptance and peacefulness.

- Mentally begin to push this blue energy up from the base of the pyramid. Feel it rising slowly until the energy flows from your head to the apex of the structure. The inside space will become a cocoon of warm, soothing, blue light. With the crystal pointed up, you will have the vibrational energy of the Earth flowing from your feet into the crystal. It, in turn, directs the energy to the peak of the pyramid. When the vibrations reach this point, the energy flows back down to your feet—a completion and a continuation.

Step Three

- Begin to focus your awareness on the crystal. Feel its texture, temperature and shape.

- Allow it to grow larger and larger until it is big enough to hold your body. Seek an entrance through its base, sides or point. Mentally project the body through this doorway. Experience a gentle pulling sensation as the transition is completed.

Step Four

- Imagine your physical self floating inside the crystal's clear white interior.

- Become the crystal by seeing, tasting, feeling and becoming aware of all the sensations.

Step Five

- When 15 minutes are up, create an exit doorway opposite from your initial entry point.

- Envision your body passing slowly through this opening. Again, experience a gentle pushing as awareness enters back.

- See the crystal growing smaller and smaller until it rests once more in your hand(s).

- Become aware of the blue pyramid of light.

- Count slowly up from 1 to 9, back to consciousness.

Reflections

Do not stay in a meditative state with a crystal

for more than 15 minutes. Later, when tolerance has been built up, this time can be extended.

Do not become discouraged if no sensations were experienced while inside the crystal or the pyramid structure. Only with practice will the abstract forces of visualization and imagination come into being.

Some days it may be impossible to drift into a meditative state. Even if the conscious chatter will not stop, benefits are still being gained by just sitting. The body and mind are in training to learn how to become relaxed.

If the energy created inside the pyramid ever becomes too overpowering, cover the crystal's point with your thumb. This grounds or cuts off the energy flow. Mentally remove the pyramid structure and resume the process on another day.

This meditation should be repeated until a degree of visualization is achieved. When ready for further development, proceed to the next exercise.

MEDITATION #3
CHAKRA OPENINGS

In order to obtain full spiritual and physical benefits from meditation, the seven chakras need to be opened.

Chakras are force centers or symbolic spots that originate in the etheric body. Some esoteric schools refer to these areas as wheels or petals. It is believed that through these openings, energy is passed from the etheric to the physical body. On an undeveloped person these centers appear to those who can see them as ". . . small circles about two inches in diameter, glowing dully."[2] On the awakened, they are bright colors greatly increased in size.

Each chakra performs a specific function and is linked to a color. The root chakra is associated with the color red. When this center is open and functioning at full capacity, the body's energy is increased. The orange of the spleen chakra when awakened will increase a person's self-worth and so on up the body until the crown chakra is reached. Some people believe there is an eighth chakra above the crown of the head which, upon opening, has the properties of pure white light, meaning it links with higher metaphysical forces (God, higher self, etc.). This chakra will not be used in this book's meditation exercises.

Refer to the following chart and diagram showing each chakra by its name, location and color vibration.

Although the awakening of each chakra is important, the third eye requires special attention, for it is linked to the intuitive center of the mind. Contrary to the connotation of "eye," there is no connection between this center and the physical eyes. It is an esoteric spot between the eyes, above the nose. This chakra is thought to be related to the dormant pineal gland which early man used to see non-solid matter. Modern man lost this ability through disuse along with most of our ancient instincts and sense

THE CHAKRAS

No.	Chakra	Location	Color
1	Root	base of the spine	red
2	Spleen	over the spleen	orange
3	Solar Plexus	above the navel	yellow
4	Heart	center of the chest	green
5	Throat	base of the throat	blue
6	Third Eye	center of the forehead	indigo
7	Crown	top of the head	violet

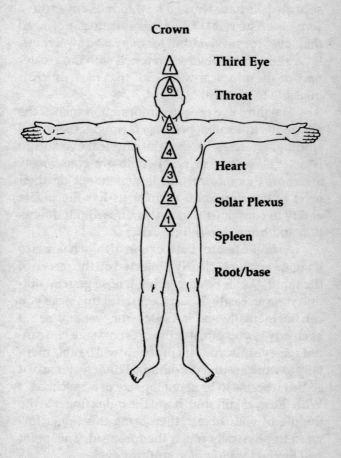

Crown

Third Eye

Throat

Heart

Solar Plexus

Spleen

Root/base

LOCATIONS ON THE BODY

awareness, but it can be reactivated. Troops in the jungles of Vietnam and prisoners in maximum-security jails have learned how to rediscover these senses for survival. The meditator does not need this "eye" for survival, but for increased awareness. It ". . . puts the individual in touch with the greater part of the physical world, all that part which is invisible to physical eyesight."[3]

The third eye picks up information such as the vibrations in a room, people's feelings, etheric and spiritual energies, all that the physical eye fails to register. Whether or not people are consciously aware of this information is dependent on their level of development. Each of us has the innate ability to consciously train this unused mind function and bring it to full capacity.

A simple test for the location of this chakra is to imagine an object clearly projected on the screen of the mind. "Let it be something whose general outline you can easily think of, even if at this stage you can not mentally 'see' it. Close your eyes and 'see' it as clearly as you can; if at the present stage you cannot achieve this, you still probably will be able mentally to work around the outline. Either way, make it so that it seems to be about the size of a matchbox."[4] With the eyes still shut, point the index finger at the middle of your object, then bring this finger forward to physically touch the forehead. This point will be the location of your third eye.

Step One

- Follow the steps in the previous meditation to the stage of holding the crystal within the pyramid.

Step Two

- Fill the pyramid with white light for protection purposes, for you are now opening up to new vibrational frequencies.

Step Three

- Mentally focus your attention on the first chakra located at the base of the spine. Imagine a vibrant, red, closed flower over this location. Gently release the petals by pushing them out through the front of the pubic bone area. In other words, envision a flower's petals beginning on the back of your spine and opening to full bloom on your front. Any number of petals can be imagined. C.W. Leadbeater in his book *The Chakras* states it is thought to have 4. When the petals are completely unfolded, move up to the spleen chakra.

- Repeat the same process with the spleen chakra, a deep, orange-colored flower with 6 petals. When it is fully opened, focus on the solar plexus, which has a 10 petaled yellow flower. Repeat the unfolding process.

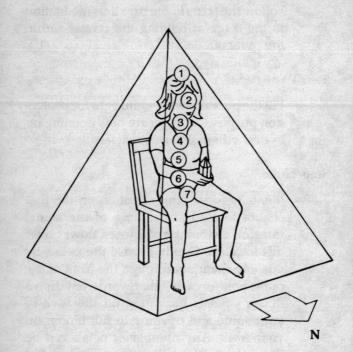

N

**OPENING THE CHAKRAS
IN THE PYRAMID**

- Move up to the heart chakra, open its 12 green petals.

- Continue up to the throat's 16 blue petals, the third eye's 96 indigo petals and finish with the crown's 972 violet petals. The actual number of petals is unimportant; the visualization and sensation of each chakra opening is what's important. Use as many or as few petals as desired.*

Step Four

- Allow your mind and body to feel a new level of awareness within the pyramid's white light.

- Focus on the crystal, and as in Steps three and four of Meditation #2, move inside your personal crystal.

- Watch for colors and/or symbols appearing.

- Remove yourself from inside the crystal after the allotted 15 minutes.

- Mentally close the petals of each chakra, starting with the crown and working down to the base. Some people believe in leaving a single red petal open on the base chakra. It is thought to never be completely closed, because this is where one of the main streams of energy flows into the body. It is a per-

---

*Reference: C.W. Leadbeater, *The Chakras*

sonal decision whether or not to leave it
open.

- Count up from 1 to 9 and release.

Reflections

The chakras are closed in order to protect you
(as a more sensitive meditator) from the negative
vibrations associated with daily living. Because these
centers have been opened up, perhaps for the first
time, you are more susceptible and sensitive to all
vibrational frequencies. The "human radio" is becoming more finely tuned.

Keep on with this meditation exercise until it
becomes second nature to open and close the
chakras. The crystal will serve to modulate these
awakened energy forces as well as helping to focus
your mind.

MEDITATION #4
FURTHER AWAKENING

This meditation will assist in awakening the
dormant intuitive forces of the third eye.

Step One

- Lie down on your back on a couch, bed
or floor.

- Place a crystal "point up" in the center of
your forehead over the third eye area. If

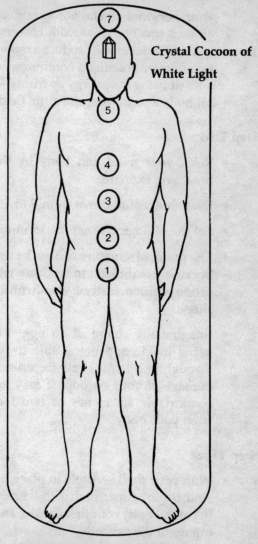

**Crystal Cocoon of
White Light**

CRYSTAL ON THIRD EYE

your personal crystal is too large, choose either a small point or a double terminated quartz. The latter will produce a more powerful effect by creating a continuous cycle of both drawing the energy up from the physical body and in from the auric fields.

Step Two

- Relax your mind and body by the deep breathing exercise.

- Eyes shut, count down from 9 to 1.

- Set the biological timer for 15 minutes.

- The pyramid structure will not be used here because it is difficult to fabricate while in a prone position. Instead, work with a cocoon shape.

- Imagine the shape of an egg. Visualize being inside and being able to look out through its opaque shell. Experiment with the size of your cocoon. It may *feel* more comfortable six inches or two feet away from your body.

Step Three

- With your shell securely in place, eyes still shut, begin to open each of the chakras starting at the base, your first chakra, and working up to the seventh.

Step Four

- Focus your center of awareness on the crystal over your third eye. Watch to see what colors and/or shapes float across the screen of your mind. In the beginning stages, you may only see darkish colored blobs drifting in and out. If nothing more tangible appears, create a dot, triangle or any simple shape. First stare at and then beyond this object. This small exercise will assist your concentration while helping to block any interfering conscious-mind thoughts.

- Relax and float with any images, symbols and/or colors that appear. They are an indication that your third eye is beginning to open up.

Step Five

- Close the chakras when the 15 minutes have expired.

- Count back up from 1 to 9.

- Remove the crystal from your forehead.

Reflections

If a cocoon shape is difficult to conceive, try imagining a roll of white tissue paper on a white sheet situated one foot over your head. Pull the paper/sheet down simultaneously over your front and back to one foot below the bottom of your feet.

Become aware of this white, translucent casing enfolding your entire body. Feel its energy creating a cocoon of protection against any negative vibrations. Some people have this structure erected around themselves at all times. The reasoning for this is: as one becomes more spiritually opened, the more prone they will be to vibrations of a negative nature.

There are several variations to this meditation. You may hold a crystal "point up" in each hand with one over the third eye. Another modification is given in the next meditation.

Always keep in mind how much power you are able to handle. If the energies become too intense, release yourself at once. When doing these more advanced exercises, it is recommended to have someone periodically check on you to ensure that all is going well. Tell this person to never touch the body of anyone who is in a meditative state and not to make any loud noises. The pain from these intrusions can be intense, causing temporary discomfort.

CRYSTAL MEDITATION #5
CRYSTAL CHAKRAS

This exercise uses crystals for enlarging the openings of the seven chakras. Seven crystals are needed, either single pointed or double terminated. Ensure that they are small enough to rest comfortably over each chakra. Adhesive tape may be used if necessary to secure the crystals.

Step One

- Lie on your back on a comfortable surface.

- Place a crystal "point up" toward your head (if single terminated) over each chakra on the front of your body.

- Mentally wrap your body in a white cocoon.

- Place yourself in a meditative state using the breathing and counting exercises.

- Set your biological timer for 15 minutes.

Step Two

- Focus your attention on the crystal lying over your base chakra. Become sensitive to its weight and temperature.

- Slowly open the red flower petals.

- Repeat this process with all the other chakras and their corresponding colors.

- Feel the energies enter and flow through these centers.

Step Three

- Mentally start pushing an even flow of white light energy from the base to the crown

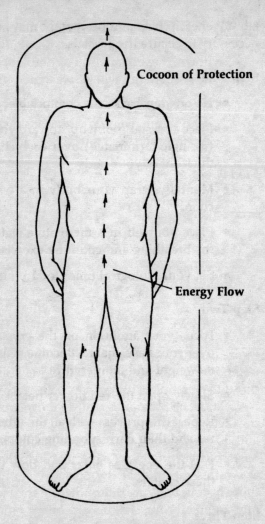

Cocoon of Protection

Energy Flow

↑ = Crystal Point Direction

CRYSTALS OVER CHAKRAS

chakra. If double terminated crystals are used, send the vibrational flow both up and down these centers. A complete circular flow of energy will be created.

- After the flow is well established, try sending different colored vibrations up through and around the crystals.

Step Four

- When the time is up, remember to close each chakra.

- Gently remove the crystals; any heavy, sudden movement can cause considerable discomfort.

Reflections

This meditation is designed to make you more aware of the body's energy points. It will also assist in the further opening of each chakra by using the directed vibration of the crystals. The heat and magnetic flux from the body stimulates the quartz, directing their energy flow in a uniform pattern (both up and down the body with double terminated crystals). If strong tingles are experienced in the chakra areas, this means that the crystal vibrations and those of your body are intermingling and balancing one another. Your chakras are being pulled into alignment.

This exercise should be repeated until all the chakras *feel* opened up. The 15 minutes can then be

Interlocking Triangles

Two Triangles Woven Together

(they are not just laid one on top of the other)

THE STAR OF DAVID

extended to 20 depending upon how well the energies are being handled.

CRYSTAL MEDITATION #6
TRIANGLES OF LIGHT

The final meditation consists of two separate exercises which will both induce higher conscious awareness.

The universal symbol of man linking with his higher self consists of two interlocking triangles. These join to form a six-pointed star called the Star of David, or Solomon's Seal.* This symbol has a deep religious significance for the Judaic people, as well as being a powerful energy pattern for performing higher consciousness work.

Separately, the lower triangle which points down, depicts the energies of man and his physical body. The second one, pointing up, relates to man's higher consciousness and his spiritual bodies. Together these two shapes join over the heart chakra interlocking in a weave.

The reader may wish to visualize this star in its three-dimensional perspective. It denotes two three-sided triangles, one above the heart and one below.

The Star of David will be used later in its entirety for healing layouts. But, for meditation purposes, the triangles will be used separately.

These triangles can be used for either raising

---

*Dr. F. Alper, *Exploring Atlantis Vol. 1*

physical energies or for a spiritual uplifting. For spiritual elevation reaching into higher consciousness, the triangle pointing up should be used. For physical help, the point faces down.

A personal crystal plus three single points are needed to perform either meditation. The setup for both is explained in the following steps.

Step One

- Place a chair or cushion in a suitable area.

- For a Spiritual Meditation,* take one of the single points and place on the floor approximately one foot away from the center of the back of your chair/cushion.

- Place one of the single-pointed crystals' point toward the chair.

- Take the other two and lay them each one foot away at the front of your chair where your feet will rest. This arrangement should resemble an equilateral triangle; a complete energy circuit.

- For a Physical Meditation,* reverse the crystals. Place one at the front of your chair, the other two at the back. The crystal at the front points toward the back of the chair. The two at the rear of the triangle point toward the front.

---

*Dr. F. Alper, *Exploring Atlantis Vol. 1*

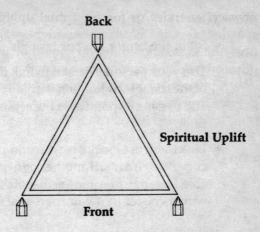

Back

Spiritual Uplift

Front

Diagram shows direction of crystal points

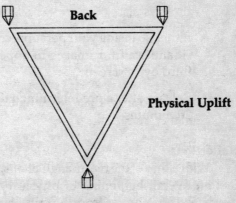

Back

Physical Uplift

Front

CRYSTAL HEALING LAYOUTS

Reference: Dr. F. Alper

Step Two

- Sit in the center of your triangle.

- Use your personal crystal to link the points of the triangle by holding it in your left hand and passing its point over the crystals on the floor.

- Link them in a clockwise direction for three complete circuits. If another person is available, have her/him join the triangle's energies with a crystal (not your personal crystal).

Step Three

- Open your chakras. Allow the body and mind to flow within the energies created by the crystals.

- Either go inside your personal crystal or just sit and wait for images to appear on your third eye's screen.

- Release after a predetermined time of 15 or 20 minutes.

Reflections

With either of the two triangulations, you should feel an overall lightening of physical and mental burdens. The energies from the crystals on the floor have created a perfect circuit of energy for you to experience this.

If possible, sit cross legged on a cushion to create a pyramid of energy with your body. A double energy force is produced.

Alternate back and forth between the six exercises until one is found that best suits your needs. Even if no mental images develop, do not worry; you are still benefiting both the physical and spiritual self. If you go to sleep while meditating, again do not be concerned. The benefits are still being received. It is the discipline and concentrated effort that counts.

When all the exercises have been tried, begin to experiment with other crystal meditation arrangements. The possibilities are infinite.

8

CRYSTAL HEALING ARRANGEMENTS

Crystal healing arrangements are performed to realign the body's energy fields, further open the chakras and to promote an overall feeling of well-being. Used in this way, they become the instruments to enhance the powers of the healer.

The first section of this chapter contains step-by-step directions on how you, as a healer, can use quartz crystal energies to facilitate healings for another person. Techniques for self-healing are described in Section Two.

SECTION ONE

How Healing Works

For the purposes of the arrangements explained in this chapter, the physical hands are never laid directly on the body. They are used to smooth out and rearrange the etheric webbing through the interaction of the healer's body energy and crystals.

The etheric body, containing the energies released through and into the chakras, will trap and retain any disharmony collected from the spiritual bodies. An experienced healer can feel these energies with his/her hands, and in some cases see them as moving color vibrations. Temperature changes and the texture of the webbing will become indications as to where more energy needs to be concentrated. For the beginning healer, discouragement should not become a deterrant if nothing is seen or felt. Healing will come with time and practice.

Crystals correct imbalanced energy; the hands concentrate and direct its flow. To be more specific, the crystals surrounding the body of the one being healed set up very specific and complex electromagnetic force fields. This energy acts to repolarize any fields that are misaligned by drawing out and adding the necessary energy vibrations to compensate for the imbalances.

The healer's physical body vibrations are added to concentrate and direct specific energy flows through the etheric body of the recipient's. If there is disease, be it spiritual or physical, a good healer will sense it either as a more intense heat or a color change, and use his/her hands to smooth over and correct the imperfections.

Responsibilities

As a healer, you should become familiar with all the possible side effects outlined in Chapter 6 before attempting any of the healing layouts.

Work with a partner closely linked to yourself, preferably a person who has worked through the meditation exercises.

You must assume full responsibility for the healings. Never leave your partner alone in a crystal arrangement. Always keep a close watch. Verbally inquire every few minutes as to whether or not s/he is experiencing any difficulties. Look for reactions of trembling, rolling of the head, chills, sweating, crying or mental disorientation. Should any of these occur, stop the session immediately by removing the crystals from around and on the body. Proceed with the treatments given below. Depending on the sensitivity of the person and the severity of the reaction(s), one or all may be needed to return her/him to a balanced state. It is very unusual for someone not to recover within a few minutes.

Treatment For Physical Reactions

Either chills or heat may be experienced as the energies within the subtle bodies realign and balance with those of the crystals . Dizziness may be felt from overexposure to crystal vibrations. Tingles, like tiny pinpricks, may be encountered in various parts of the body. These are all indications that the energies are still working on healing an ailment such as a backache, cramps, headache or sore muscles. To treat:

1. Cover the person with a blanket to hasten the return of normal body temperature.

2. Have her/him lie still for at least five minutes.

Then, inquire as to whether or not reactions are still occurring. If so, sprinkle a few drops of water on the wrists and forehead to help the person return to normal. If desired, the feet and forearms can be massaged to increase blood flow.

3. Have your partner slowly get up.

Treatment For Emotional Reactions

After the session, the person may cry, appear to be mentally disoriented or feel inadequate to deal with any surfaced negative emotions such as fear, hate, lack of self-worth or jealousy. You, as the healer, must help her/him understand that the crystals have triggered the release of old negative blocks that were wedged into the emotional and mental bodies. Tell the person that this is a positive reaction and encourage the emotional release. Talk, comfort, listen and proceed to help her/him return to a more balanced state of mind by closing the chakras.

1. Have the person lie on their back on the healing surface.

2. Touch the crown chakra with your index finger of the hand connected to the intuitive portion of your mind.

3. Verbally instruct her/him to visualize with you the closing of the purple-colored petals associated with this center. Your energies combined with the person's will cause this closure to occur instantaneously.

4. Repeat the same touching and visualizing with the third eye's indigo and the throat's blue petals.

These actions shut down the energy in the person's spiritual centers. Now a full return to the physical state of awareness needs to be facilitated.

5. Place both hands, palms down, fingers slightly spread, directly on his/her solar plexus (at the navel area).

6. Slowly begin to move your hands down the body in a gentle pulling motion over the abdomen, spleen, and base chakras, to the joints where the legs meet the pubic bone area. Keep on drawing this etheric energy down both legs to the feet. This process needs to be done only once. You are effecting the exit of excess emotional energy from the lower chakras out through the body.

7. Shake the excess energy from your hands.

8. Have the person sit up and begin to move around.

Another treatment to rid the person of feeling out of touch with reality and self without using the pulling motion is to follow steps one through five, and then:

6. Place an index finger directly on the solar plexus while you and your partner visualize its yellow-colored petals growing roots down to the spleen center.

7. Place a finger over the spleen and *feel* its orange petals growing roots down to the base center

8. Visualize the red energy moving down the legs, into the floor and out to the Earth.

This grounds the person to the physical plane, linking the lower chakras to the energies of the Earth. Any time one feels spaced out, too spiritual or out of touch with the "real" world, this energy connection can be made.

A final alternative to restore balance between the spiritual and physical aspects is to have the person take a walk outdoors, preferably in a park, along a beach or a rocky area. The lower centers need to be imagined as reaching down into the Earth. The person may even wish to lie prone on the ground to quickly return the mind and body to its normal state of existence.

Preparations for Your Healing Treatments

Before commencing these layouts, remove any metals such as belt buckles, coins and crystal jewelry. These objects can cause interference and distortion of the energy fields. The person on whom the healing is to be performed should either loosen or remove any restrictive clothing.

As in meditation, a peaceful, dimly lit environment is preferable. If desired, soft music may be played to eliminate any distracting sounds and to relax your partner.

It is recommended that you inform the other person exactly what will be taking place. Advise her/him to let you know immediately if any physical or emotional discomfort is experienced.

The ideal direction for working with any crystal configurations (whether it be in meditation or healing) is north to south. The head should lie to the north with the feet pointing to the south. The direction of the crystal flow must be reversed in the Southern Hemisphere. The concept behind this arrangement is to align the body with the Earth's magnetic field and to enhance the flow of the crystal energy. Unfortunately, the electrical circuitry in the average house/apartment alters and negates any practical advantage of lying this way. However, if you are using crystals away from electrical wiring and equipment, then the healing effect will be amplified by using a north-south arrangement.

The person to be healed should lie on their back flat on the floor or healing table. Arms are placed comfortably at his/her sides with the feet slightly apart. This person may choose to close their eyes and go into a light meditative state for greater relaxation. The more at ease the person is, the more benefits will be gained from the treatments.

HEALING ARRANGEMENT #1
THE STAR OF DAVID

For the first configuration, 6 single points and a generator crystal are required. The sizes of the points can vary within a couple of inches of one another.

In Meditation Exercise #6, two separate triangles were used to induce a spiritual and physical uplifting. These triangles will now be linked to create the full power of the Star of David configuration.* You, the healer, will be stimulating the crystal energies by linking their points with a quartz generator. This will establish an even flow of energies through the crystals.

Step One

- Place one of the points approximately six inches above the center of your partner's head.

- Place the other two crystals on the outside of both knees, six inches away from the body. All crystal points are directed upward toward the head. The first triangle is now completed.

Step Two

- Place a crystal, point up toward the head, six inches away from your partner's feet, making sure it directly lines up with the head crystal.

- Place the two remaining crystals (points up) at the side of each elbow. The two triangles will not be perfectly equilateral, but their energies will function as such.

---

*Dr. F. Alper, *Exploring Atlantis, Vol. 1*

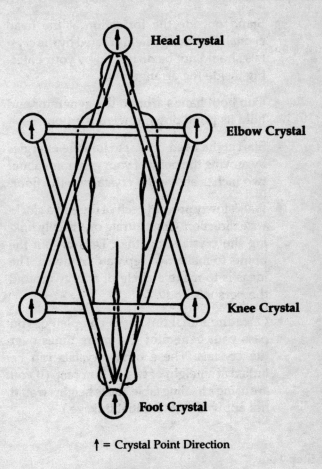

Head Crystal

Elbow Crystal

Knee Crystal

Foot Crystal

↑ = Crystal Point Direction

BODY OVERLAY
FOR THE STAR OF DAVID

Reference: Dr. F. Alper

Step Three

- Stand outside the formation at the head crystal. The energy field created by the crystals should not be disturbed by your entering inside the arrangement.

- Cup both hands around the generator and hold its point down toward the floor.

- Start at the head crystal to join the energies by moving the point of your generator about two inches above the crystals on the floor.

- Walk slowly around each of the 6 in a clockwise direction. Concentrate on visually linking the crystals together. Do not join the points to make two separate triangles. The ideas is to make a circle of energy around the person's body.

- Once the initial linking is completed, you pass your generator five more times over the crystals. These other crystals can be linked at a height of two to four feet. (If you are using a healing table, these heights would not apply after the initial linkage.)

Step Four

- Place your generator aside.

- Watch your partner for any reactions and verbally ask whether or not s/he is comfortable with the new energies.

- If all is satisfactory, leave this person in the configuration for no longer than 10 minutes.

Step Five

- Remove the crystals from around the body in any order.

- Have the person lie still until s/he feels ready to get up.

Reflections

The linking of the crystals creates a seal around the body being healed. A transference of energy takes place by flowing out of the healer's body into the generator crystal which in turn activates the other 6 with the circular motion. The more times the generator is passed over the crystals, the more the energy will be amplified. A good guideline to follow is to circulate the generator as many times as the number of crystals in the arrangement.

All points of the quartz in the Star of David are directed toward the head, with the head crystal pointing out away from the body. This is to facilitate an energy flow from the base chakra to the crown which assists in creating higher consciousness.

A clockwise linkage was suggested since this rotation corresponds with the Earth's magnetic flow in the Northern Hemisphere.

In Chapter 2 it was stated that crystals charge one another by energy directed into their base and sides which spirals out the point into the next crystal where the same process is repeated. The healer may have observed that only the left side of the configuration had the energy flow directed in this manner. The right side, due to the clockwise rotation, had the reverse occur with energy seemingly flowing from the points down to the bases. This is not the case because the crystals correct the energy flow by themselves. The very fact of laying them out with all points up creates this proper flow. The circulating generator caused the crystal energies to flow back and forth in all directions for a completely contained field.

Upon completion of a crystal healing, the recipient may experience a slight disorientation for a few minutes. The healer should try and gain as much insight as possible as to what has occurred both physically and spiritually to the one being treated. A follow-up should be done to learn how the energies are being coped with.

The recipient should not be exposed to any other crystal arrangements until the first healing has been repeated at least four more times. In these beginning stages, healing should only be performed once a week. Tolerance to the energy vibrations needs to be built up slowly. The body and time need time to adjust.

HEALING ARRANGEMENT #2
THE DOUBLE STAR OF DAVID

"The twelve-pointed star is perhaps the single

most powerful configuration that one can use to form a pattern of energies for healing."[1] The Double Star of David's twelve points depict the universal number of completion. This arrangement will totally integrate the energies of the physical and spiritual bodies. This double star raises vibrations to a higher level. There is nothing in the physical or spiritual self that is not affected by this healing configuration. It is a total cleansing and realignment of all energies.

The healer will be more physically involved with this second arrangement because the hands will be used as part of the healing process.

The palms of the hands can be effective healers with or without the presence of crystals. In this second healing arrangement, assistance will be generated from both the crystals' and the healer's energy fields. Through experimentation, one hand may be found to be more adept at feeling energy changes in the etheric webbing of the person being treated. The opposite hand may be better at smoothing and spreading out this energy over the recipient's body, or that both hands placed one on top of the other creates a balanced effect.

With healing, each hand produces different effects. The left produces the soothing, calming energy while the right instills healing powers. A mother will automatically place her left hand over a child's forehead to ease the distress of a fever rather than her right. The beginning healer should experiment with the effects of the hands and then decide which method to use.

A word of caution: use this twelve-star pattern only on a partner who has already built up a tolerance to crystal energies. Watch carefully for any signs of a negative reaction and if one occurs, remove the crystals at once.

This arrangement requires 12 single points and a generator. As in the previous exercise, the person to be treated lays flat with arms down at the sides. The crystals all "point up" for higher vibration energy and are placed approximately six inches away from the body in the following manner:

- A crystal above the center of the head.

- A crystal at the feet, lining up with the head crystal.

- A crystal beside the left shoulder.

- A crystal beside the right shoulder.

- A crystal beside the right elbow.

- A crystal beside the left elbow.

- A crystal at the right wrist.

- A crystal at the left wrist.

- A crystal at the right knee.

- A crystal at the left knee.

- A crystal at the right ankle.

- A crystal at the left ankle.

THE DOUBLE STAR OF DAVID

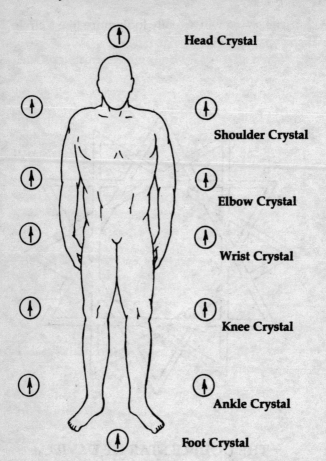

↑ = Crystal Point Direction

CRYSTAL LAYOUT FOR THE
DOUBLE STAR OF DAVID

Reference: Dr. F. Alper

The shape will actually look more like a circle than separate equilateral triangles.

When all is set up, commence with Step One.

Step One

- Hold the point of the generator a few inches away from the crystals around your partner's body and begin to link the 12, starting at the head.

- Slowly work around the circle in a clockwise direction, holding the generator about two inches away.

- Repeat the circuit for 11 more times. Mentally visualize the circle of energy flowing as the generator is rotated over the crystals.

Step Two

- Set the generator aside so the energy field is not diverted.

- Stand beside the circle, never inside it. A central spot to stand is parallel to your partner's solar plexus area.

- Extend your hands, palms down, over his/her solar plexus. In the beginning stages of learning how to use the hands to move crystal energies, it is helpful to bend over your partner. Hold your hands about six inches away from his/her body. More sensations will be felt at this distance.

Step Three

- With your palms down, concentrate on feeling the buildup of energy over your partner's body. After a few minutes, your palms may start to tingle. If nothing occurs, it simply means you are not consciously aware of the energies. Be assured, they are there.

Step Four

- Slowly move your hands over the entire body without touching your partner.

- Walk around to ensure all areas are being covered. Spread the energy with your hands. Think of it as polishing a wooden surface back and forth, and around in slow, circular movements. Try experimenting with different movements and positioning of your hands.

- Keep moving the field over the entire body. If any inconsistencies, blockages or color changes are perceived, concentrate the energy with your hands over these areas.

- If nothing is felt or seen, keep spreading the energy for a couple of minutes.

Step Five

- Remove your hands after the energy field has been evened out.

- Ask the person how s/he is feeling. If all is positive, leave the recipient in the formation for five more minutes.

Step Six

- Remove the crystals.

- Leave your partner lying down until s/he is ready to get up.

Reflections

Some beginning healers will not experience any energy tingles in their hands, see colors or feel any alterations in temperature. These sensations will come with practice and self-development.

In time, the healer will be able to sense and correct any blockages in the recipient's etheric body. A buildup or lack of energy can be felt. Dark color shadings in the webbing may be visualized. Tears or holes may be perceived. All of these aspects can be smoothed over with the crystals' energies and the healer's hands.

Healing abilities differ with each person. Some people prefer to use a generator crystal for healing instead of the hands to amplify the effects. Others like using their hands as these are more delicate instruments than crystals. A quartz may be substituted for the hands in these arrangements. Per-

sonal experience and testing will decide which is
more effective for the healer.

The Double Star of David may be repeated in a
week's time. The actual number of minutes in this
formation may be increased to a maximum of 15.

The one receiving the crystal treatments may
experience some side effects. These reactions are
indications that spiritual and physical bodies are
adjusting in order to assimilate the crystal energies.
They are to be expected as part of the development
process. When this person feels capable of taking
more power, the treatments may be done every
four days. His/her mind and body need at least 48
hours to adjust.

HEALING ARRANGEMENT #3
THE CHAKRAS

This configuration will further assist in opening the chakras. It follows the same concept as
Meditation #5, but is more powerful due to the
increased number of crystals.

The Double Star of David is combined with
crystals over the chakras for realignment and removing blockages. The crystals will create a directed flow of energy from the feet straight up the
center of the body and out the crown. In an undeveloped person or one who is just beginning to
open up to higher consciousness, these chakras are
often blocked. For example, a person may be having
difficulty seeing colors or symbols through the

third eye center. The healing arrangement can help to unblock this chakra.

As the healer, you should become aware that new energies are being funneled in and out of the one receiving the treatment. This requires close attention to ensure that the person is not experiencing any difficulties. If so, refer to Treatments for Physical and Emotional Reactions found on page 89 and 90.

To perform this layout, 12 single points, 7 double or single points plus a generator crystal are required. The 7 crystals should be small enough to lay comfortably on the body. Once the person is lying down, the following steps should be performed.

Step One

- Follow the instructions in Healing #2 for laying the 12 crystals around the body.

- Before linking these, place 7 small crystals over each of the chakras. Ensure they are in a straight line up the front side of the body as follows:

- A crystal on the root chakra.

- A crystal on the spleen.

- A crystal on the solar plexus.

- A crystal on the heart area.

- A crystal on the throat.

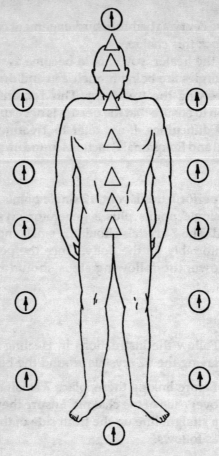

↑ = Crystals Around the Body

△ = Crystals on Chakras

CHAKRA HEALING ARRANGEMENT

Reference: Dr. F. Alper

- A crystal on the third eye.

- A crystal at the crown.

If single points are being used, all should have their points up. If the crystals start to roll off any of these centers, secure them with a small amount of adhesive tape. Because the crown chakra can be difficult to place a crystal on, it is suggested to place a small book between the head crystal of the initial 12 and your partner's head. Place the crystal on the book so that its base is just touching the crown.

Step Two

- Link the outside 12 for 12 rotations with your generator.

- Run the generator from the feet straight up the center of the body over the chakra crystals to the head quartz.

- Link down from the head along the chakra crystals to the foot quartz.

- Do this up and down connection 6 more times.

Step Three

- Place the generator aside.

- Stand beside your partner outside the formation parallel to his/her solar plexus area.

- Using your hands, palms down, begin to evenly distribute the energies.

- Try and find any uneven areas over the body and focus more energy to these spots with your hands (or crystal).

Step Four

- Inquire as to the condition of your partner and if all is well, leave this person in the configuration for 10 more minutes.

Step Five

- Ask your partner to close up each of the chakras as the crystals are being gently removed. Do this beginning with the crown, and ending with the base.
- Remove the circle of 12 outside crystals.

Reflections

Depending upon the recipient's needs, this exercise may be repeated or alternated every week with other healing arrangements. Every time a healing is performed, the one receiving these energies steps closer to inner awareness.

HEALING ARRANGEMENT #4
CLUSTERS

Clusters are powerful instruments in alleviating any emotional buildup from excessive negative stress. They work effectively within the circle of 12 by throwing off their sporadic energies into the circle and drawing back consistent energies at the same time. Clusters rid the body of negative vibrations while feeding it back ones of a more positive nature.

This healing arrangement requires 12 single points, 3 clusters and a generator. If at all possible, the clusters should be of graduating sizes that are comfortable enough to place directly on the body.

As in previous arrangements, the one to be healed lies on a flat surface. When this person is comfortable, proceed with Step One.

Step One

- Place the 12 crystals around his/her body.

- Put the largest of the 3 clusters over the pubic bone area (the root chakra).

- Place the second largest on the solar plexus.

- The smallest goes over the third eye area.

Step Two

- Link the outside crystals in the usual manner.

- Link the 3 clusters by running your generator up and down the full length of your partner's body three times.

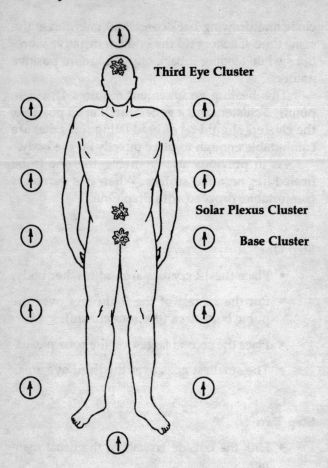

Third Eye Cluster

Solar Plexus Cluster

Base Cluster

↑ = Crystal Direction*

CLUSTERS WITHIN
THE TWELVE CRYSTALS

*Direction reference Dr. F. Alper

Step Three

- Place your generator aside,

- Use your hands to spread the energy field over the body. Do not attempt to smooth these vibrations, as the clusters are giving off inconsistent energies.

Step Four

- Check to ensure the recipient is comfortable with the newly created energy fluxes.

- Let the person lie in this arrangement for 15 minutes.

Step Five

- Remove the clusters in any order.

- Remove the outside 12 crystals.

Reflections

A common reaction to this cluster layout is for the recipient to experience either chills from the body releasing excess energy or intense heat from its absorption. These temperature fluctuations will pass after the healing has been completed. The benefits, as stated earlier, will be an alleviation from the emotional stress. The crystals over the three chakras will stimulate further conscious awareness by a further opening of these centers.

HEALING ARRANGEMENT #5
THE ARRAYS

The final healing arrangements are the arrays. These layouts may be done separately around the head or feet, or be combined for an overall healing.

Often when opening oneself up to newer levels of awareness, a person can experience difficulties in relating to everyday life situations. Work, relationships, anything to do with the here and now can become of secondary importance. A grounding effect is the recommended remedy in order for this person to be able to live an evenly balanced spiritual and physical life. This pulling of the "head out the clouds" is achieved through using the feet array.

If the person is well grounded to the physical world, awareness of the spiritual self may be expanded through the head array. This layout will assist this person to become more in tune with vibrational frequencies other than those found in the three-dimensional world. Through regular usage of this configuration, intuitive powers will be enhanced.

The feet and head arrangements can be combined to achieve an equal balance of both the physical and spiritual aspects of life. This crystal layout will also assist to further open and align the chakras.

These three layouts are described below starting with the feet array.

Feet Array

To set up this arrangement, 7 single points plus 2 generator crystals are required. As in the previous exercises, the recipient lies flat on the floor on his/her back.

Step One

- Take 7 single points and place them approximately four inches from the body as follows (all points out away from the body):

- A crystal between the two feet.

- A crystal beside the left ankle.

- A crystal beside the right ankle.

- A crystal at the left calf.

- A crystal at the right calf.

- A crystal between the left ankle and the foot crystal.

- A crystal between the right ankle and the foot crystal.

- A healing crystal (of a fairly large size) is placed six inches away from the center of your partner's head, point up. It must be in line with the quartz between the feet.

Step Two

- Link the crystals with your generator, starting at the right calf.

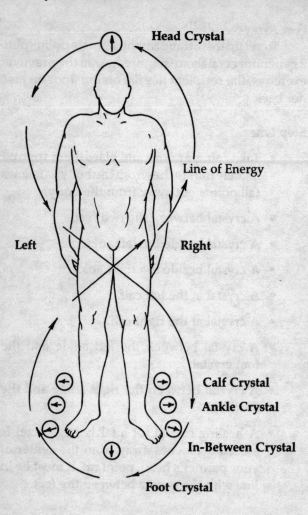

Head Crystal

Line of Energy

Left

Right

Calf Crystal

Ankle Crystal

In-Between Crystal

Foot Crystal

↑ = Crystal Point Direction

FEET ARRAY

- Continue the circuit to the right ankle, then to the next crystal until the left calf is reached.

- Draw a line of energy with your generator over to the base chakra, then to the right side of your partner's body.

- Extend this energy field up to the right side of the head crystal. This energy is then circulated down the body in a figure-eight fashion from the left side of the head crystal to the right calf.

- Repeat this same circuit six more times.

Step Three

- Do not use your hands to smooth out or spread the energies.

- Leave your partner in this array for 15 minutes.

- Remove the crystals in any order.

Reflections

The energies are uneven in this arrangement due to not having the controlling circle of 12 crystals. Instead, a figure eight of energy has been established by linking the feet to the base chakra and then the head. The energy circuits down again over this chakra to the feet. Most of this energy is concentrated in the feet to help ground the person by pulling the vibrations down into his/her body.

The field is then diverted up through the base chakra. This center is the main trigger of all the other chakras as it holds and releases the body's life forces. The excess energy flows out through the head crystal. The circuit down to the feet again ensures that the energy is evenly balanced.

The healer does not use the hands to spread or smooth out the energy as it is not evenly distributed over the body by the nature of this configuration.

This array may be used twice a week if needed. It can also be alternated with other healing arrangements.

Head Array

The head array requires 7 double terminated and 2 generator crystals.

Step One

- Have your partner lie on his/her back in the usual manner.

- Place the 7 double terminations around the head in a halo fashion four inches away from the body.

- A crystal at the center of the head.

- A crystal at the left ear.

- A crystal at the right ear.

- A crystal at the left side of the chin.

- A crystal at the right side of the chin.

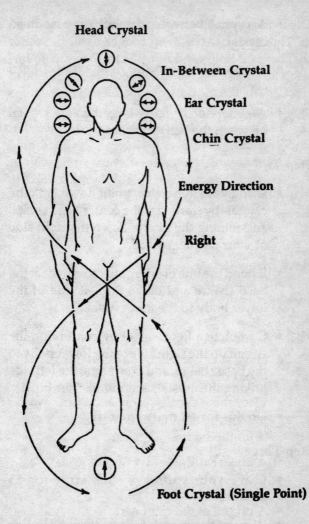

Head Crystal

In-Between Crystal

Ear Crystal

Chin Crystal

Energy Direction

Right

Foot Crystal (Single Point)

↕ = Double Terminations

HEAD ARRAY

- A crystal between the left ear and head crystal.

- A crystal between the right ear and head crystal.

- A generator or fairly large healing crystal between the feet, point up.

Step Two

- Using your generator, point down, link the crystals by starting at the center head crystal and joining the quartz down the right side of your partner's head.

- Extend the line of energy to cross over at the base chakra and down the left side of the lower body to the foot crystal.

- Complete a figure eight by continuing the circuit up the right side of the lower body to the base chakra, and then along the left side linking the crystals around his/her head.

- Do this for six more circuits.

Step Three

- Leave your partner in this array for 15 minutes.

- Remove the crystals in any order and let this person rest for a few minutes. A lightheaded feeling may be experienced.

Reflections

The crystal placed between the feet pulls the vibrations in a downward direction to alleviate some of the concentrated energy around the head. It creates a grounding effect as well as a linkage point for the base chakra. The double terminated crystals both pull in and release their energies around the recipient's head. The person is automatically replacing any lost energy with higher vibrational frequencies.

Upon completion of this healing, a meditation is recommended for the recipient. This person is already open to receiving new frequencies and can easily go into a deep, meaningful meditation.

This array should only be done on a weekly basis due to its powerful effects on the mind. With all configurations, the recipient needs time to adjust.

Combination Feet and Head Array

For a completion of the physical and spiritual aspects, a combination of the feet and head layouts may be used. This effect will realign and balance all energies.

To perform this healing, 7 single points, 7 double terminations, and a generator crystal are required.

Step One

- Place the crystals around both the head and feet as shown in the two separate arrangements. No grounding crystals are required.

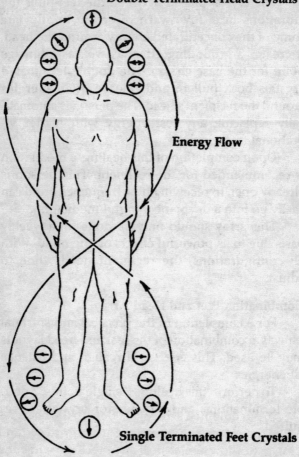

Double Terminated Head Crystals

Energy Flow

Single Terminated Feet Crystals

↑ = Crystal Point Direction

COMBINED HEAD AND FEET ARRAY

Step Two

- With your generator point down, link the crystals around the head by beginning at the center quartz and joining the crystals down the right side of the feet array.

- Keep the line of force moving around the right side of the feet crystals.

- Pass over the base chakra and link up the array on the left side of the recipient's head.

- This figure eight is joined 13 more times.

Step Three

- Do not use the hands.

- Leave your partner in this arrangement for 15 minutes.

Step Four

- Remove the crystals in any order.

Reflections

This combined array will open up the energies of the three upper chakras: the throat, third eye and crown, to allow a release of any blockage while the person still remains grounded to the physical world. The figure eight connects all the crystals to cause their energies to flow from top to bottom and back again.

This array may also be used within the circle of 12 crystals. Because it causes an extremely powerful energy flux, it should not be used on someone who has not been exposed to several months of crystal arrangements. The healer and recipient should collectively decide on the usage of this powerful combination.

SECTION TWO

Self-Healing

Some of the above healing layouts can be done without the assistance of a partner. The same prerequisites apply: a quiet environment, no restrictive clothing, removal of crystal jewelry, setting the internal biological clock to return full alertness after 15 minutes and cleansing the quartz in the sea salt solution after each healing.

The difference between self and partner healing is the absence of "healer's hands" to direct and concentrate the vibration flow. Instead, mind thought and body energy when combined with the crystals' natural healing properties will generate a similar effect.

To ensure a complete energy connection and to maximize the harmonizing qualities of the crystals, the following general steps should be used for all self-healings.

Step One

- After placing the crystals in a predetermined pattern, stand inside the configuration holding a programmed generator, point directed down. Link the energies for as many rotations as there are crystals.

Step Two

- Place the generator outside the crystal arrangement, at least one foot away so the magnetic field is not distorted.

Step Three

- Lie down, face up in the configuration and open all chakras by following the instructions given on page 67 of the Crystal Meditation.

Step Four

- Focus your mind on the base chakra. Visualize a beam of white light forming and then traveling up the center of your body, connecting to the crown chakra.

Step Five

- When this energy force reaches the crown, mentally spray it out like water from a fountain. Imagine the white light running from the head crystal to the shoulder crystals, to the elbows and so on until all are connected.

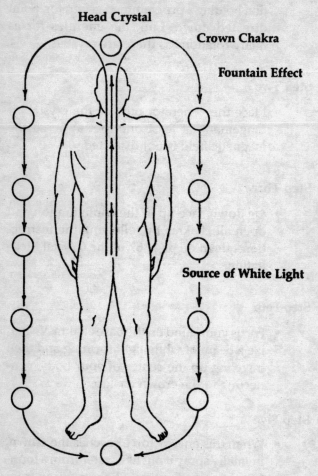

Head Crystal

Crown Chakra

Fountain Effect

Source of White Light

← = Direction of Flow

**MIND THOUGHT
TO CONNECT ENERGIES**

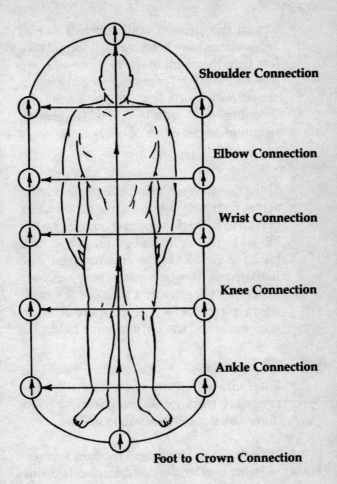

Shoulder Connection

Elbow Connection

Wrist Connection

Knee Connection

Ankle Connection

Foot to Crown Connection

↑ = Crystal Point Direction

CRYSTAL CONNECTION

Step Six

- Repeat this process until you feel that all connections have been made. It should take less than three minutes. For those who are sensitive to crystal energies, a tingling, warm sensation may be felt. Simply having the thought of making the linkage will be enough to complete the circle of energy.

Step Seven

- Using the same white beam, link the current across your body by joining the left shoulder crystal to the right shoulder quartz, the left elbow to the right, and so on to the final union of the foot to the crown crystal. The hookup has now been made between your generated energies and those of the crystals to completely encase the space between your body and the outside force field.

Step Eight

- Enter into a meditative state and allow the crystals to work at realigning any imperfections contained in the subtle bodies.

An alternative to this "mind thought connection is to first lay out the crystals, then stand outside the arrangement as in the partner healings. A generator is passed around the quartz for the same number of times as there are crystals. They are left undisturbed for 10 to 15 minutes to build up a magnetic force field. Your entrance will cause a slight rupture in the energies, but you can reconnect the seal by passing your left or right hand, palm down, over the hole.

HEALING ARRANGEMENT #1
STAR OF DAVID

This configuration may be used for emotional or physical healing of the self. Six single points and a generator are required. Either lay out the crystals ahead of time or follow these steps:

Step One

- Take 3 crystals in your hands and lie on your back on the healing surface.

- Reach above your head and place one crystal point up about four inches above the crown.

- Sit up, leaving your legs flat on the surface and place a crystal beside each knee, points directed up. This completes the upper triangle of the Star of David.

Step Two

- Take the remaining 3 crystals and place each point up with one between the feet, four inches from the body, directly corresponding with the head crystal.

- The other two are put outside each elbow. This is the lower triangle of the Star of David.

Step Three

- Use the generator by standing inside the Star. Hold it point down to link the energy field.

- Repeat the circuit for five more times.

- Place it aside, as far away from the layout as possible. Lie down and begin to make the mental energy connection.

Step Four

- Allow yourself to drift into a meditative state after setting your internal clock to return to full consciousness after 15 minutes.

Step Five

- Sit up slowly.

- Mentally close all chakras (refer to Chakra Meditation p. 71).

- Remove the crystals in any order, either while still inside the pattern, or from outside the layout.

This pattern will assist in gently realigning the subtle bodies while initiating you to crystal energies. It may be repeated after 48 hours.

HEALING ARRANGEMENT #2
THE DOUBLE STAR OF DAVID

This layout should only be used after there has been exposure to the single Star of David, as it affects spiritual and physical energies. If any physical reactions such as tingles or temperature variations become too intense, remove yourself from the energy by sitting up, thereby breaking the circuit. If emotions begin to surface such as repressed anger, hate or even love, try and flow with them. However, if they become too intense, release yourself from the crystals. Any reactions indicate that the mind and/or body is giving up a subconsciously suppressed condition to allow new harmonizing vibrations to flow in. You may not experience any overt feelings, but be assured that alterations of a positive nature *are* occurring.

Twelve single points and a generator are required for this layout. The crystals should all point up to allow a complete flow of energy. They are placed approximately four to six inches away from the body.

Step One

- Lie down and place the crystals singly around the body or estimate where they would fall of you are outside the pattern (refer to page 100 for the exact location of each).

Step Two

- Connect the energies from either inside or outside the circle with a generator.

- Make the linkage for 11 more times.

- Place the generator aside.

Step Three

- Lie down on your back.

- Open the chakras, enter into a meditative state and direct the flow of energy around and over your body.

Step Four

- Try and allow any sensations to flow without censoring or stopping.

- Return to full alertness after the present time of 15 minutes.

- Remove and cleanse the crystals.

Allow at least 48 hours for the energies to assimilate and harmonize before commencing any further treatments.

HEALING ARRANGEMENT #3
THE CHAKRAS

This arrangement is used to help open a blocked or unstimulated chakra. It is not recommended that all seven centers be covered with crystals at the same time without the aid of a partner. The vibrations from the quartz, on and around your body, may cause reactions that you are not ready to handle.

If a chakra is not fully functioning, a crystal is placed directly over it, along with the outside pattern of 6 or 12. The Star of David will facilitate a slow, gentle release of energies while the Double Star augments healing power. If you feel capable of handling even stronger energies, double terminated quartz may be substituted for singles.

If the third eye is not giving you satisfactory access to inner visions, colors or meaningful meditations, it needs crystal stimulation. A single point is placed over this center while you are lying in the Star or Double Star (7 crystals are needed for the Star and 13 for the Double Star). The layout directions are:

Step One

- Follow the instructions in Arrangement #1 or #2 for placing the crystals around the body.

Step Two

- Link the outside quartz with a generator.

- Place it aside.

Step Three

- Lie down in the configuration and place the extra crystal over the third eye.

Step Four

- Set your internal clock to return you to full awareness after 15 minutes.

- Enter into a meditative state, focusing your attention on the third eye crystal.

Step Five

- Exercise the energies of this center by feeling the weight of the crystal, noting its temperature, mentally visualizing it sinking into your skin, and becoming part of your physical being.

- Keep repeating this process, trying not to let your mind wander onto other thoughts.

Step Six

- Return to full awareness.

- Close all the chakras.

This layout may be repeated in 48 hours. If no changes appear to be happening (e.g., colors, visions, symbols are not manifesting), then you are simply not ready to receive this information. Persevere with the exercise. In time (which varies for each of us), this center will open up.

The arrangement can be used on any chakra. If your heart is blocked to receiving or giving love, then the outside pattern would be used with a single point placed over the heart center. If the throat is blocking you from communicating inner feelings to others, place the crystal over the throat chakra. Always be guided by your inner self as to what needs to be worked on. As you begin to advance awareness, you will become more in tune to physical and spiritual needs and be intuitively directed to the appropriate crystal healing.

HEALING ARRANGEMENT #4
CLUSTERS

This pattern requires 12 single points, 3 clusters and a generator. It readily generates healing vibrations with the clusters automatically distributing energies on and around the body.

Step One

- After connecting the energies of the outside crystals with a generator, gently place the largest cluster (about three inches base diameter) over the root chakra.

- Place another over the solar plexus and a small cluster on the third eye (refer to page 112 for diagram).

Step Two

- Open all chakras and mentally connect your body to the outside crystals.

- Run a white beam of light up and down the center of your body from feet to crown to link the clusters' energies.

Step Three

- Enter into a meditative state, setting your timer for 15 minutes.

Step Four

- Gently remove the clusters in any order.

- Close the seven centers.

As with all crystal arrangements, allowance for the mind and body to assimilate new energies of at least 48 hours should be adhered to before repeating or administering a new layout.

Summary

The healing arrangements given in this chapter are just a few of the limitless configurations that are available to assist in raising conscious awareness. The layouts will hopefully spark new ways of working with various crystal configurations. The healer should always cautiously experiment with additional techniques. It is suggested that the healer not perform new arrangements on a partner until personally tried with documented results.

The crystals only supplement the power of the human mind and energy fields. Therefore, they are only tools and are effective as their owner is. You may reach a time in your development when crystals will no longer be needed to assist you in a healing capacity, for you will have become a perfectly clear, functioning, balanced energy force.

9

COLOR HEALING

Color awareness occurs at many levels. Each color the eyes see, the mind reflects on, has a profound effect on the emotional and mental aspects of our being. When choosing particular colors for our decor, clothing, jewelry or cars, we are expressing a need to enhance or change an emotion(s) at a conscious or subconscious level. For example, decorating a room in soft hues of blue promotes a peaceful, serene ambiance. What we are doing is surrounding our aura with the energy of color to soothe, calm or maintain a mood. A decor in reds or hot pinks indicates a desire to stimulate sexual or earthly "real" world energies. Yellows and oranges increase creativity, self-confidence and courage.

Paintings can invoke repressed emotions. The dark, lifeless colors of winter storms or raging sea scenes move us to surface and release depressing thoughts. Bright and cheerful pastel shades lighten our mood, providing an outlet for feelings of being too bogged down from daily life problems. We therefore use our external surroundings to reflect internal feelings and needs.

Choices of gemstone jewelry are much more subtle than just "liking" the color. Wearing a blue, such as lapis lazuli, reflects an inner need of wishing to communicate with others more effectively. A string of tumbled rose quartz worn over the heart chakra is indicative of a desire to increase our capacity to love and be loved. Emerald or jade colored gems bring the green rays of healing into our aura. Rubies, garnets, and bloodstones replace a loss of vitality. Every stone in the mineral kingdom brings a healing vibration of a physical and emotional nature into our energy field.

Clothing shades are also a reflection of our inner mood. A yellow colored dress or shirt shows a need to stimulate our creative abilities. Wearing red can signify inner strength and power, or the desire to create these attributes. Orange indicates the need for courage, green for healing and balance, and blue for peacefulness. When soft shades of violet or indigo are chosen, we are desirous of drawing in vibrations for spiritual illumination. White, the sum total of all colors, is indicative of a quest for purifying the mind, body and soul.

Whether it be a room, painting, gemstone, car or piece of clothing, if our intuitive self is allowed to choose the color, we can discover a great deal about our inner feelings. This is all part of the process to advance our consciousness; being aware of what is transpiring at all times in our physical, emotional and mental bodies.

To understand what color *is* and why it has subtle effects on us, its properties need to be examined.

Color Properties

Visible colors in the third dimension are energy vibrations or rays emitted from the center of the electromagnetic spectrum. When light is passed through a prism, a rainbow of seven colors appears. Each projected ray has a specific wavelength and vibrational quality (see diagram).

The lowest and longest vibration is red. It is followed by a shorter ray of orange, then yellow, blue, indigo, to violet, the highest. The rays on the lower end of the spectrum are associated with the physical energies of survival, sexuality, anger, self-worth, courage and vitality. The upper colors are related to the higher aspects of unconditional love, communication and spiritual enlightenment. The degree to which emotional and physical effects are experienced depends on the intensity and type of ray filtering into our auric field. (Refer to the table on page 55 which depicts colors and their properties.)

Red, the color that activates the energies of the base chakra, is the lowest on the spectrum. Its properties are extremely "Earth oriented," being our connection to the physical world. Red heals problems related to the lower parts of the body such as the legs, rectum and colon. Concentration of this vibration on the pubic bone will help to increase our

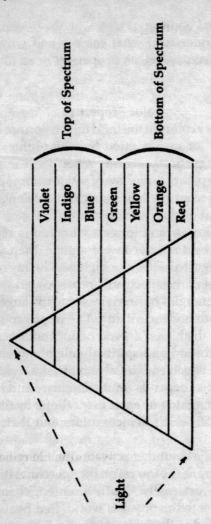

PRISM EFFECT OF COLORS

energy level, connect us back with the materialistic world if we become too spiritual, and release feelings of anger and depression. Red signifies vitality, life and physical healthiness.

The next color, *orange*, brings healing vibrations to the sexual organs. Menstrual cramps and conditions related to the reproductive organs can be helped when this ray is applied to the spleen chakra. Feelings of lack of confidence, unworthiness and fear can be transformed into confidence, self-acceptance and courage with its usage.

Yellow, the last of the lower colors, relates to the energies of the solar plexus. It stimulates increased mental activities such as reasoning and creative thinking. Body parts that are healed by this ray are the stomach and abdomen.

The *green* ray is the midpoint of the light spectrum. Its properties are growth, regeneration and overall mental, emotional and physical healing. Green is the focal energy bringing the upper and lower colors and their associated chakras into harmony and balance. It works directly on the heart chakra, increasing our capacity to love by filtering jealousy, hate and resentment from our auric field.

Green is referred to as the overall healing color grounding us to the "real" world while enhancing inner awareness. Any physical, emotional or mental problem can be helped when its vibrations are applied.

The rays of the upper spectrum, blue, indigo, and violet are linked to spiritual rather than earth energies. *Blue* instills tranquillity and has the properties to help us express our true feelings when talking with others. It is the color that can soothe any tormenting emotions while healing conditions of the larynx and thyroid.

Indigo blends the serenity of blue with the violet of higher consciousness. It stimulates the intuitive aspects of the third eye center. Indigo's healing properties can alleviate tension headaches and overall body stress.

Violet, linked to the crown chakra, is the last of the seven rays. It helps us to tap into higher consciousness, giving the feeling of total oneness with all aspects of self, man, Earth and the universe. Violet can be used for an overall emotional and physical healing.

Pastels, derived from combining and adding white to the initial colors of the spectrum, can be used to sustain or further stimulate conscious awareness. Shades of pink, magenta, lemon, purple, gold, turquoise and rose are just a few of the colors that can be created. If there is desire to be in perfect harmony with all aspects of the physical and spiritual self, hues of lime (a combination of white with green), pink (white with red) or amber (orange with white) may be used.

In order to benefit from the seven basic colors or pastels, we use colored or clear quartz instilled with color to heal physical and emotional problems and to raise us above the limitations of our current consciousness. As mentioned in Chapter 2, there are several varieties of quartz, some of which are smoky, rose, amethyst and citrine. Each colored crystal plays its own unique role in this New Age, assisting in our search for higher levels of mind, body and soul perfection.

Colored Quartz

Colored quartz can be used for healing and meditation purposes. It can be used simultaneously with clear quartz because of having the same crystalline structure of spiraling triangles. Selection, programming and cleansing techniques are exactly the same.

The following usages of these stones are in no way conclusive. These tools are capable of healing and raising our levels of awareness no matter how or where they are placed in our auric field.

Smoky Quartz

Smoky quartz ranges in color from grayish to brownish black and is available in clusters, double terminated and single points. Its energies alleviate problems linked to the base chakra. By placing a single stone over this center or meditating with it in the hand, the following benefits can occur:

- Its vibrations increase the desire to succeed in the materialistic world by activating any lost instincts for survival. This property makes smoky quartz especially helpful to those people who have suicidal tendencies due to giving up on trying to find a job or career.

- By reinforcing the feeling of being in a physical body, it helps us accept the fact that we are tall, short, thin, fat, male or female instead of experiencing dissatisfaction with our given body structure.

- It assists people who have their spiritual centers opened to the point of being out of balance with the lower chakras by making them aware of their body's existence. They tend to ignore the reality of having a physical structure which needs taking care of.

- This crystal helps overcome depression and severe mood swings by absorbing negativity from the aura.

- For those people prone to psychic attack from negative persons or forces from other dimensions, smoky quartz will work to dissolve this vulnerability.

- Our elimination system can be stabilized whether it be constipation, a fear of letting go; or diarrhea, a fear of retaining and holding.

This crystal can be used as the foot quartz in the Star or Double Star of David patterns to help cleanse negativity from the subtle bodies. The clear and smoky crystals all need to point down rather than up for this to take place. If energy/vitality is required, use the smoky quartz in either layout with all crystals pointing up.

Only one smoky quartz should be used in the

early stages of working with this energy. Its numbers can be increased for meditation or healing after the energies have been fully assimilated by the mind and body.

Amethyst

This crystal varies from a purplish blue to almost a white color. Because it represents the violet ray of light, it is often referred to as the Spiritual Crystal associated with the third eye center. It is found in single points, clusters and geodes which are large slabs of quartz taken directly from the mine. The following changes can occur by using it directly over the third eye, holding while in meditation or substituting for clear quartz in healing layouts.

- It directs the mind away from mundane, recurring thoughts, taking us into the deeper recesses of our subconsciousness during meditations.

- Amethyst activates the third eye to be a receiver of visions, colors and symbols. Some people will be able to "see" spiritual guides, have precognitive sight and generally be more intuitive.

- It creates feelings of comfort, lessening inner stress and tension.

- This purple color helps remove boredom, the thoughts of having no direction or purpose and a lack of spiritual growth.

- Physically, it eases tension headaches and relieves sore eyes.

To obtain the maximum benefits from amethyst, lie in a single or Double Star of David and place either a small cluster or single point (directed up) over the third eye. The healing is then performed in the regular manner of using a generator, hands of a healer or self-healing techniques.

Rose Quartz

Rose quartz, a pale pink chunk or single point is called the "love crystal." Its energies are directly linked to the heart chakra, having soft, feminine vibrations. Rose quartz is extremely beneficial to us when placed directly over the heart chakra in healing layouts. If a single point is used, it should point up. It can be worn around this center as a tumbled quartz necklace. In today's impersonal society, we can never be exposed too much to its comforting, loving vibrations.

It increases our ability to give and receive love. Some of us may feel unworthy of accepting love from others because we do not love ourselves. Through prolonged use of this crystal, we can begin to open up to the inner beauty of ourselves. When we have self-love, others will be attracted to our radiating, pure energies.

With this crystal, we can obtain a sense of freedom from negative self-doubts and gain inner peace as we let go of all destructive thoughts. We feel better about who and what we are. No longer will there be a need to agonize over the reason for our existence, because the soul's knowingness will have become part of consciousness.

Citrine

This crystal varies from yellowish gold to light brown. Its yellow ray is found in clusters, double terminated and single points. Citrine works directly on the solar plexus chakra. For healing, it can be placed over the navel or around the entire body as a substitution for clear quartz in the patterns of 6 or 12.

The following benefits will occur:

- It helps improve the digestive system and reduce the tendency to have ulcer flare-ups.

- Citrine absorbs fears and the tense feelings that occur in the stomach when we are upset.

- It restores lost confidence.

- This stone stimulates intellectual and creative activities.

- It promotes a happier disposition towards life.

- The yellow ray can increase or level off an unhealthy appetite.

If colored quartz is not available or if there is not an intuitive attraction for it, colors can be projected into clear crystals. This alteration makes these stones just as powerful as the naturally colored quartz for healing and meditation.

Clear quartz permits absorption of the color rays. Gels, lights colored slides or mind thoughts are just a few of the methods to increase the crystal's capacity for more intense healings and deeper meditations.

Quartz can be coated with special colored gels. Natural sunlight or a soft electrical light can be directed through a translucent sheet of colored paper which is placed around the crystal. Carousel slides can be shone directly on the quartz. With any of these methods, a few minutes of contact is required for a color absorption into the spiralling crystalline structure. When the healing or meditation is complete, the crystal is held in the hand while the thought of pure white light is visualized and passed through it. This returns the quartz to its original clear state. If using gels, soak the stone in sea salt and water for approximately ten minutes to remove the surface color. The white cleansing light is then projected through it.

Crystals can be programmed with a specific color property using the same concept as described in Chapter 4. It is held in the left or right hand. The mind beams out the thought of instilling into the crystal structure the healing color of red, green or whatever is needed to effect an emotional or physical cure. Just by visualization, the color will be programmed into the crystal.

These "colored" crystals may be substituted as healing tools around or on the body for gemstones or naturally colored quartz. In place of lapis or sapphire which opens a blocked throat chakra, blue can be instilled into a clear quartz which is then placed over this center. If a person has stomach problems, a yellow colored crystal would replace citrine to help soothe the solar plexus. For an overall healing, green may be programmed into the crystals before being placed in the pattern of 12. For heightened meditation, a personal crystal can be instilled with the color violet instead of using an amethyst for spiritual illumination. Simply use the color that corresponds to what is needed to improve the emotional or physical condition.

Some further suggestions for colored crystal work are given below.

Balancing the Body Energies

To help balance the chakras in the pattern of 12 (Double Star of David arrangement), project red into the crystal placed between the feet, orange for the two that lay beside the ankles, yellow at the wrists, green at the elbows, blue at the shoulders and violet at the crown.

Proceed to spread the energies over the one being treated with the hands. Leave her/him in this configuration for 15 or 20 minutes. Clear the colors from the crystal with the sea salt solution and white light.

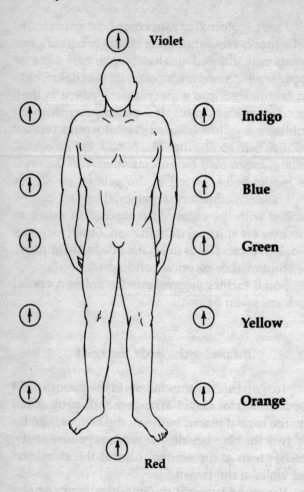

↑ = Crystal Point Direction

BALANCING BODY ENERGIES

Chakra Opening

Colors corresponding to the chakras may be programmed into 7 crystals before placing them directly on the body. Using the exercise described on page 106, red is put over the base, orange for the spleen, yellow on the solar plexus, green or pink for the heart, blue covers the throat, indigo over the third eye, and violet at the crown. The healing is then performed in the usual manner.

Spiritual Growth

To assist in giving a spiritual uplifting when a person feels out of touch with his/her higher self, the crystal pattern of 6 or 12 may be colored with indigo or violet. The crystals are placed around the body, and a similarly colored generator is rotated over the layout to link the energies.

Grounding

To bring a person in touch with everyday life (as opposed to spiritual uplifting), red, orange or yellow may be used around the body in a pattern of 12 or 6. This colored layout pattern should be used only if there is a feeling of being out of touch with reality. Often when questing for higher awareness, normal life situations tend to become unimportant. Since a balance between the spiritual and physical must always be kept, grounding may be required.

Love Vibrations

If an individual is overly aggressive, has self-anger, or is easily upset by situations or people,

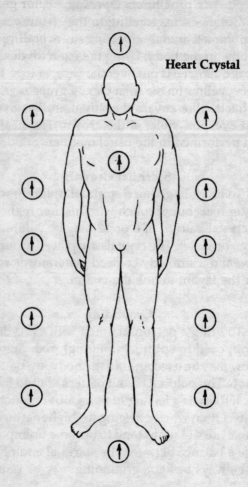

Heart Crystal

↑ = Green Colored Crystals

LOVE VIBRATIONS

clear quartz programmed with the color green or pink will assist in removing any negative emotions from the aura while effecting an overall physical healing. The pattern of 12 is instilled with either color, plus one crystal needs to be placed on the heart chakra. Its point is directed up toward the head (see diagram). The healing is performed with the usual spreading of energies by the healer's hands, or can be self-directed. The one being treated should enter into a meditative state to further assist the release of negativity. Green and pink rays are the love vibrations, soothing and restoring positive energies in the aura.

Conclusion

On a final note, as with any crystal application, inner guidance should always be adhered to. You, as the healer, will be directed to know when to use the right colors.

10

CRYSTAL JEWELRY

This chapter elaborates on Chapter 4's information regarding the wearing of crystal jewelry. Instructions are given for making pendants, a Star of David amulet, bracelets, ankle bracelets and a crystal headband.

Wearing jewelry set in precious and semi-precious stones is an ancient tradition. Throughout the centuries, literature has perpetuated the significance of jewels by analogies like emerald seas, turquoise skies, ruby lips and sapphire eyes. The Old Testament (Exodus 28, verses 15-21) recounts the directive for making a twelve-stone breastplate to be worn by the priests of Israel to increase their powers while performing sacred duties. The lost Egyptian, Phoenician, Mayan, Indian, Atlantean and Lemurian races adorned their bodies with jewels for many reasons that remain yet undiscovered. It is believed that the stones were used for their attractiveness, to enhance the wearer's beauty, as gifts of eternal love, for currency, religious purposes, protection against evil spirits, indications of social status, healing, good luck charms, to increase psychic powers, stimulate the chakras, magnify telepathic thoughts, and in pendulums which were used as hypnotic and dowsing instruments.

Today, men and women carry on the ageless custom of wearing jewelry made from rubies, lapis lazuli, emeralds, jade, opals, pearls and many other gems. Also, in this Age of Aquarius, the wearing of crystals has been reintroduced for many New Age purposes. Quartz jewelry balances the subtle bodies, energizes the chakras, protects against negativity, cleanses the aura, enhances spiritual growth, attracts other Children of Light, and any other special tasks its owner wishes to program into the stone.

A two-way relationship transpires when quartz is worn next to our skin. The crystal receives a continuous charge from heat expelled by the body. This keeps its electrons in an endless state of excitement, perpetually releasing the embedded program. We, in turn, use the crystal's power to discharge negative thoughts and emotions from our aura, increase our vitality and advance our awareness— all of which helps us to develop a more positive outlook toward ourselves and life. Personal experience has shown that this blending of energies will take place after 15 days of contact between the crystal and our body.

Crystal jewelry can be programmed to protect its wearer from the negative vibrations emitted by people or circumstances. The projected mind thought creates a solid wall of energy around the subtle bodies allowing for only the positive, loving vibrations to filter through. This protection is very crucial to those who are in the beginning stages of consciously advancing their levels of awareness, as sensitivity to all vibrations is heightened.

The quartz may be programmed to increase spiritual consciousness, heal a physical disease, release an undesirable thought/emotion, or whatever the wearer's current needs are. The possibilities are unlimited.

To program crystal jewelry, the instructions in Chapter 5 should be followed. Cleansing in sea salt and water needs to be performed on a regular basis. Since the crystal is constantly within our auric field, it readily picks up any of the impurities and negativity contained within our physical, emotional and mental bodies. These will be amplified back, actually accentuating the problem(s) if the crystal is not kept cleansed. If you have been in a situation where there was an argument, around sick people, or near people not compatible with your vibrations, remove and soak the jewelry. Base the immersion time on the amount of negativity you intuitively feel was absorbed. It may require an hour to a maximum of two days. Be guided by your inner voice. After cleansing, run cold water over the stone to stimulate its electromagnetic energy. The final step is to pass white light through the crystal. All of this is done without removing the crystal from its setting. The salt will not be harmful to the metals around the stone. If it is a crystal necklace, made entirely of quartz pieces strung together, ensure at the time of purchase that the string is a plastic material and not thread. The ones made with thread will rot more readily.

Periodic soaking of at least every two weeks is needed to remove the oils that are picked up from the skin. The jewelry is then energized on a cluster or placed in direct sunlight for a few hours.

If wearing a necklace, pendant or amulet, judge whether or not it should be worn outside or inside your clothing. When in a situation where the vibrations are loving, intellectually stimulating or serene, you may wish the crystal(s) to absorb this energy. They would then have to be worn outside. If, however, you desire to only have them influenced by personal vibrations, always wear the jewelry next to your skin.

Types Of Jewelry

Crystals can be worn as rings, bracelets, ankle bracelets, earrings, necklaces, pendants, amulets and headbands. Copper, gold or silver are the suggested mounting metals. All increase the electromagnetic energy contained within the quartz. Copper, however, is the most compatible with our body energy and is the least expensive to purchase. Its molecular structure absorbs our natural metallic wastes while amplifying the crystal's power. Because this metal is in its pure form, copper is a natural conductor of the Earth's magnetic energies. Like the molecular structure of quartz, electrons move freely through it. When wrapped around a crystal, copper acts as a conductor channeling and directing the electromagnetic power released from the quartz, acting as an energy booster.

Rings, Bracelets, Ankle Bracelets and Earrings

When wearing any type of crystal or gemstone jewelry, the etheric, emotional and mental bodies are being influenced by the healing powers of the stone. Reflexology, which arouses dormant passageways from the etheric to the physical structure, can be replaced by the use of crystal jewelry. Having constant stimulation on particular centers will open up the energy flow from the etheric to the physical.

A ring increases the energy emission of quartz. For instance, if insertion of healing power is done with the right hand, a ring placed on this side will further amplify your healing energies. Or, if the left side of the body is weaker than the right (those who are right handed will find the left side weaker), wearing this jewelry on the left hand will help at the etheric level to compensate and balance the energies.

Bracelets have the same enhancing effects as rings to increase the strength of the weaker body side. Medically, the wrist contains one of the main pulses connected to the heart. Metaphysically, it is linked to the heart chakra. If there is a need to increase the capacity to give and/or receive love, then prolonged wearing of a crystal bracelet will increase the heart chakra's force. It also brings an overall calming effect to the wearer. It should be a personal decision as to which wrist the bracelet is worn on. Try it on one side for a few hours and then the other to discern which is most effective.

The ankles are associated with the lower centers, and the wearing of a crystal anklet can ground a person by strengthening the link to the physical everyday activities of life. It works on the base, spleen and solar plexus chakras while healing any problems related to the sexual organs, hips and lower back.

Earrings will maintain the body's energy equilibrium after balance has been achieved on both sides of the body. Spiritually, any ear problems such as earaches, buzzing or dizziness that don't have a medical explanation can be attributed to not "hearing" what others are really saying or not heeding your intuitive higher self. Wearing crystal earrings will bring in the necessary healing energy to help open you up to listening to the real meaning of both spoken and unspoken words.

Necklaces

Crystal necklaces made of several small chunks or a single quartz will help to remove blockages and ailments in the throat area. The person who has difficulty verbally expressing her/himself due to sputtering or stammering would find that a necklace helps to stimulate this chakra, giving confidence to the act of speaking. If there is a hesitation to communicate truth for fear of hurting another or a lack of self-worth, s/he will discover that the right words can be spoken through activating this center. Finally,

String of Quartz

Crystal Bracelet

CRYSTAL JEWELRY

Quartz Ring

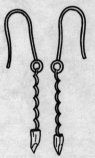

Crystal Earrings

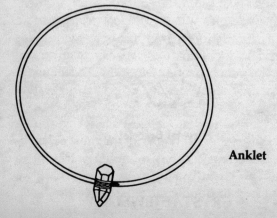

Anklet

a sore or irritated throat can be soothed with a crystal necklace.

If wearing a single stone, it needs to fall directly over the throat chakra. Its size should be less than two inches for comfort reasons, using a single, cluster or double terminated quartz. The chain's length should be 14 to 16 inches. Some people will experience energy tingles or heat around the throat, indicating the crystal is at work. Others will not feel any overt sensations. But be assured, the quartz is opening and aligning this center.

Pendant

The heart is the center of our two halves. It is the division between our upper spiritual centers and the lower physical and emotional aspects of our being. This is the recommended chakra to wear a crystal over to effect a perfectly balanced you. The higher and lower centers are automatically influenced by its energies. When the heart chakra has a constant stimulation from quartz, it encourages self-love and increases our capacity to give and receive this much needed emotion. The pendant also acts as a shield, protecting our auric field from negativity.

Copper is the best metal to use for wrapping around the crystal, although not the most aesthetically pleasing since it has a tendency to tarnish quickly. The chain can be gold or silver with a single, cluster or double terminated crystal.

Amulet

Amulets were traditionally designed as charms to protect the wearer against evil forces. In the ancient civilizations of the Egyptians, Romans and Druids, amulets were believed to possess magical and religious powers. They were shaped into hearts, scarabs, eyes, serpents, gods and goddesses made in brilliant gemstones. It was the cultural innuendo placed upon the jewelry that empowered the person, and not necessarily the object. Modern-day amulets are found in symbols of crosses, zodiac signs, Buddhas, cosmic eyes and pyramids.

This type of protective charm can be made using a crystal as its focal point. Its energy is similar to the pendant, and is most beneficial when worn over the heart chakra. When programmed, the amulet can bring specific powers to its owner. For instance, if you give the crystal the image of attracting positive light forces, increasing your luck, speeding your initiation into higher awareness or shielding you from negativity, the amulet will then hold that intent for you. What the mind thinks, it believes.

Making a Necklace, Pendant and Amulet

One need not be a skilled craftsperson to make crystal jewelry. Rock shops and lapidaries sell rings, necklaces, pendants, bracelets and amulets at inflated prices. Their pendants and necklaces tend to be capped with gold or silver material which can deplete the maximum benefits of the crystal because the base is covered.

The following directions will assist you in creating your own jewelry for less than a few dollars. The chain for around the neck can be made of copper, gold or silver, but the wrappings holding the crystal need to be in copper.

Materials needed are a pair of needlenose pliers or tweezers, twenty-gauge copper picture wire, and a crystal of less than two inches. It is recommended that a single point be worn initially rather than a double terminated or small cluster to allow a slow integration of crystal and body energies. The point should be intact and may either point up for spiritual development, or down for grounding to the physical aspects of yourself. Instructions are given below for a single and double terminated pendant or necklace.

Single Point

1. After cleansing and programming the crystal, cut a piece of copper wire about nine inches long.

2. Place the crystal on the midpoint of the wire as shown, as close to the base as possible.

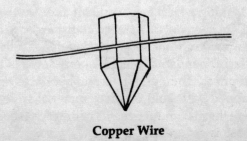

Copper Wire

3. Wrap each end of the wire around the crystal for at least six turns, leaving the base uncovered and the ends of the copper free. The more times the metal is wrapped around the body of the quartz, the more power it will elicit.

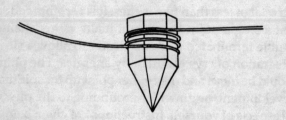

Wrappings of Copper

4. Bend the ends of the wire into small circles, large enough to fit a strong chain through. After the chain is fitted, close each end of the copper. The chain will fall behind the copper.

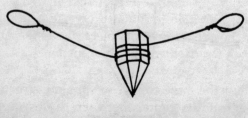

Chain Holes

5. The finished product will look like this.

Direction for Physical Grounding

Direction for Spiritual Uplifting

Double Terminated

1. Place a double terminated crystal of less than two inches on a nine-inch piece of copper after it has been cleansed and programmed.

2. Follow the same copper wrapping instructions, but begin in its center, between the two terminations.

3. The finished product will look like this.

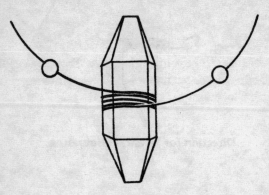

Amulet

Amulets can be any symbol. The one described below is the Star of David with a crystal in its center. The shape is symbolic for fully developing both aspects of life, the physical and spiritual. The crystal will empower the triangles by connecting these two forces.

A small, single point of less than one inch is needed.

1. Cleanse and program the crystal with the desired thought.

2. Cut two pieces of copper wire, each about four inches long.

3. Bend them into two separate, three-sided triangles. The base of each will need to be interwoven to close the triangle.

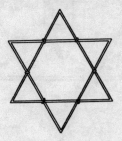

4. Place one over the other to create a Star. Take bits of copper wire to secure where the points meet by wrapping or using a bonding glue.

5. Suspend the crystal in the center of the Star by wrapping it with wire following the instructions for making the pendant, but leave enough wire to hang it down from the top of the upper triangle so it falls directly in the center of the amulet. And, make a notch to suspend the chain through.

6. The finished product will look like this.

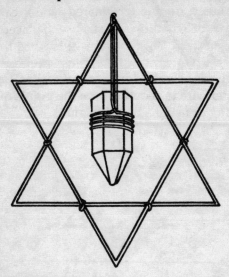

Making a Crystal Bracelet and Ankle Bracelet

As with the pendant and amulet, copper is the preferred metal to use for the band of a bracelet and anklet. It is easily molded into shape and magnifies the energies of the quartz while absorbing toxins from the body.

Bracelet

Twenty-gauge copper picture wire, pliers or tweezers and a seven-inch thick rolling pin, glass pop bottle or any type of cylindrical mold are needed to make this piece of jewelry. The suggested crystal size is a one and one-half-inch double terminated quartz. Because of being located at the wrist, it can be safely used to stimulate the heart chakra of even an initiate without the risk of side effects. As stated previously, double terminated quartz can be too intense for a first-time crystal user if placed directly over a chakra. This crystal will balance the subtle bodies while gently stimulating the heart center. Instructions for making the bracelet are as follows:

1. Cleanse and program a one and one-half-inch double terminated crystal.

2. Cut three separate pieces of copper wire, at least one inch larger than your wrist. For instance, if your wrist measures six inches around, cut the wires to seven inches.

3. Bend the wires into three circles. An easy way to ensure this shape is to wrap each circle around a rolling pin or any circular shape that is slightly larger than your wrist. The bracelet has no adjustable clasp, so make certain it can slide over your hand.

Rolling Pin

Three Wires

4. Close each circle by one twist with the pliers or tweezers. This will leave each with two end pieces for wrapping the crystal

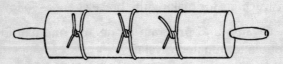

Twisted Wires

5. Still on the mold, move the three wires so they are one-half inch apart with the twisted ends facing you.

½ Inch Apart

6. Place the center of the crystal over the middle wire and secure with the ends of copper by twisting them with the pliers a couple of times. Cut the left-over ends at an angle so there are no sharp edges to catch in your clothes.

Crystal

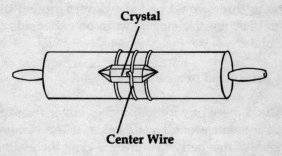

Center Wire

7. Adjust the upper and lower wires so they are beneath each termination (not point) of the crystal. Then secure and cut the ends. The finished product will look like this:

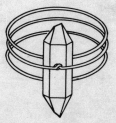

8. Slide the bracelet off the mold and onto your wrist.

Ankle Bracelet

The same round mold is required to construct an anklet. The instructions are given below using a single point measuring less than one inch, although a double terminated crystal can be substituted. Only one strand of copper wire is needed for the band as three would be too awkward around the ankle. The jewelry may be worn on either side of the body.

1. Cleanse and program your crystal.

2. Cut a piece of wire four inches larger than the measurement around your ankle. If the circumference of this part of your leg is eight inches, the wire needs to be 12.

3. Use a rolling pin or similar shape to mold the wire into a circle, leaving three inches free at one end, one at the other.

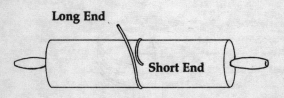

Copper Wire

4. Take the long end (the three inches) and wrap it around the body of the crystal for at least two turns.

The crystal should be secure with the end of the wire entwined in the wrapping.

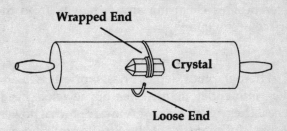

Wrapped End

Crystal

Loose End

5. Decide if the crystal point will face up toward your head, or down to the ground when worn on the body. Remove the anklet from the mold and place it around your ankle.

6. Hold it in the position of your choosing and taking the tweezers, secure the loose end of copper to the wire that is wrapped around the crystal. To remove the anklet, simply use the tweezers to loosen the short end. Your finished jewelry will look like this:

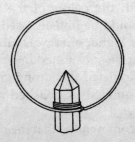

Copper has a tendency to tarnish faster than gold or silver. Soaking the entire piece of jewelry in salt and water will return this metal to its original luster besides cleansing any negativity from the surface of the quartz.

Headbands

Hieroglyphics depict priests, priestesses and other influential figures wearing jeweled head-pieces. The ancient ones were aware of what powerful surges of energy could be attracted into the aura by placing this type of jewelry over the center of the forehead. In our current age, we are just beginning to discover the significance of enhancing the third eye chakra. With stimulation, this sixth center brings us clarity of thought, telepathic messages, past life information, clairvoyance, symbols, colors that are more brilliant than those found in the third dimension, deeper meditations, intuitive abilities, and a host of other spiritual attributes. Having the third eye stimulated with a quartz headband will, over a period of time, increase the wearer's level of awareness.

The stone can be clear quartz or amethyst (associated with the colors of the third eye). A single point should be initially used with its apex pointing up for higher energy. Double terminated quartz can later be substituted once the body and mind have assimilated the strong energies of the single point. Tumbled or polished amethyst may also be used.

It is not recommended that the band be left on

for more than five minutes in the beginning stages of experiencing its energies. Dizziness and disorientation may be felt. Allow at least one week of wearing once a day for the suggested time before increasing to ten minutes. Always use caution. The goal is not to push yourself into higher conscious states, but to slowly and sensibly allow this natural progression to happen.

The headband is most effective when used in a meditative and telepathic capacity. (Telepathy is described in Chapter 11.) Directions for making the band and a corresponding meditation are given below.

Making the Band

Once again, copper is the most effective material to energize the quartz. Natural fabrics such as silk and cotton may be substituted but do not create a circle of power around the head. All they do is hold the crystal in place. The tools needed to make the copper version are pliers and twenty-gauge copper wire.

1. Select either a tumbled amethyst, single clear point or amethyst point of approximately one to one and one-half inches. Cleanse and program the stone. One suggested thought is to receive clearer information from your intuitive center. Visualize your third eye opening on the etheric level and unblocking messages from your higher self.

2. Measure the perimeter of your head, slightly above your nose. This is where the band will rest.

3. Cut a length of copper four inches longer than your head measurement.

4. Place your stone in the center of the wire and wrap it tightly with the copper for a minimum of three turns.

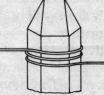

5. Bend the remaining wire to form a circular shape.

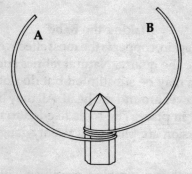

6. Measure one inch from the end of wire A. Using a pair of pliers, bend it into a small loop and engage its end into the same wire so there is a closure. Cut the wire on an angle so it is not sharp.

7. Hold the band around your head, making certain that the crystal is located in the center of your

forehead. Estimate how much copper will be left over when the headpiece is fitted. Place your thumb on the excess wire and remove from your head.

8. Taking the end without the loop (B), bend it into a hook.

9. Link the hook into the circle.

10. Unhook and place around your head. The finished product will resemble this:

What you have created is a continuous flow of energy from the crystal, around the head and back to the crystal with no disruption to the power field.

Meditation

This exercise will assist you to become comfortable with the energies of the headband. The meditation needs to be performed while sitting in a chair, feet flat on the floor or in the lotus position.

Step One

- Charge the crystal in the band by holding it for a few moments.

- Secure the headband around the forehead.

- Relax mind and body with the breathing techniques given in Chapter 7's Crystal Meditations.

- Set your biological clock for five minutes.

Step Two

- Focus your attention on the crystal headband. Feel its weight and the slight pressure of the copper.

- Begin to mentally push energy from your feet, up the center of the body (along the kundalini) and out into the crystal.

Step Three

- Envision a line of blue energy streaming from the crystal, around the copper wire and back to the stone in a clockwise direction. Repeat this movement until you physically begin to feel either the crystal heating up or the band becoming tighter.

Step Four

- Relax and wait for images, messages, or whatever information you are meant to receive, to come to you. Nothing may manifest during the first few tries, but be assured your third eye is receiving stimulation.

Step Five

- At the end of the five minutes, remove the band. If you wish, soak it in sea salt and water if negativity was released. Repeat the same process for the next few days, gradually increasing your time.

If any discomfort is felt during the meditation, remove the band at once. Do not resume the exercise for at least twelve hours.

11

FUTURE AWARENESS

The latent intuitive mind can be accessed through crystal meditations and healings. As the bridge begins to narrow between the subconscious and conscious state, there will be a union of all aspects of the spiritual and physical self. When the etheric body relays positive messages to its physical counterpart, the body becomes the perfect temple for housing the mind.

Many changes will occur indicating growth. Questions such as why life is so complicated and the reason for your being here will begin to fall into perspective. The silent voice within becomes heard, listened to and is allowed to guide the newly awakened mind with a knowingness that can be trusted. A new and positive outlook toward everyday situations will occur. Nature with her renewing revitalizing forces will become an integral part of your life, giving it an increased sense of balance. There will be a coming together of like minds, a sharing of knowledge, truth and understanding. All facets of self and its relationship to the outside world will begin to flow in a harmonious balance.

There may come a time in your growth when the vibrations of crystals are not as important for development as they were initially. They should not become your only area of expression. Until then, use them as a vehicle to greatly enrich your life and growth process.

This chapter will introduce some advanced crystal applications as "food for thought" to further stimulate your mind. Practical usages for quartz energies are also given to assist in raising the vibrations of your daily life.

Further Healing and Meditation Work

Crystal meditations offer access to the right, intuitive portion of the brain, and healings are an expression of this spiritual and physical awareness. In any type of arrangement around the body, try and keep the number of crystals to either 3 (as in the triangulation for spiritual/physical upliftings), 6 (the Star of David), or 12 (in the Double Star of David). These figures are based on the trinity of expression symbolizing growth, higher consciousness and completion. Changing this ratio can produce distorted force fields. In correct three-dimensional perspective, all set up energy fields that amplify and enhance the healing and meditative powers of the crystals. When placed directly on the body, they need not be restricted to specific numbers, for the energies within the body are being worked with and manipulated rather than the outside overall auric field.

As one becomes more aware and sensitive to vibrations, certain sound frequencies (either natural or synthetic) will trigger reactions. Each of us has a special note or frequency that our inner self resonates with. The senses become heightened. Chills or energy tingles will often run up and down the spine. When this sound is discovered, humming, singing, chanting or playing it to crystals will amplify their effectiveness.

Some metals, especially copper, magnify crystal energy. Grid works of the Star of David and other configurations constructed to draw in the Earth's magnetic fields will assist in higher consciousness work. However, it is strongly recommended that these be left until such a time as a tolerance and understanding of crystal energies has been well established.

In whatever crystal applications you work with, whether it be with sound, color or new layouts, always be directed by your inner voice. It will guide you correctly. For if you were not ready to work with these energies, they truly would not be available for you. Never try and force other people to use crystals. It may not be the right expression for them. You may educate and then let them come to you for assistance. Each person must awaken from sleep at his/her proper time.

Removing Electromagnetic Energies

Most of us live in a network of heavy electromagnetic energies. Electrical wiring, steel structures, appliances and electronic devices surround our auric fields at home and work. As you become more developed, your sensitivity to these unnatural forces tends to increase, which in turn causes these distortions to affect you in a negative fashion. Take a compass and watch how magnetic north fluctuates, in some cases up to 80 degrees, when it is placed in different areas of your home.

Crystals placed in the four outer corners of the home will help to eliminate these distortions. Use single points of at least two inches in length, their points directed outward. Instill each with a program to move these detrimental energies out of your living quarters. Cleansing and recharging will be required at least every two weeks to maintain their effectiveness.

Property Protection

The same number and size can be embedded in the four outer corners of your property. The bases are planted in the ground with the points exposed to the air. These light tools need to be programmed to repel the energies of any unwanted intruders such as sales people and robbers. A wall of energy will build up, protecting your home from undesirable people over a period of a few weeks.

Auric Cleansing

Single points of less than three inches can be placed in each of the four corners of the bathtub or shower. If a heavy amount of negativity has been encountered from stressful situations or after performing an intensive healing, you can cleanse your aura from the water and by directing the crystal's points away from the tub. If a revitalizing of energies is needed, turn the points inward while you bathe. The crystals may be put either in the bath water or along the ledge of the shower area.

Drinking Water

A small chunk of crystal can purify water of etheric pollution when placed in the bottom of a nonmetallic container filled with tap water. Allow it to remain undisturbed in a quart container for twelve hours. The stone's energies will neutralize any psychic impurities in the water. When drunk, this crystal clear water will perform a wonderful cleansing process in our bloodstream. Any natural remedies such as vitamins, gem and flower elixirs will be enhanced if taken with crystal water. You will no longer need to purchase treated water.

If symptoms of an approaching cold or flu are felt, increase your consumption of this water to build your auric defenses and natural resistance. This same water can be used for cooking vegetables, making hot beverages, washing the hands and face, and watering plants.

Plants

Small chunks can be buried in the soil just beneath the surface of household and potted plants. There is an immediate exchange with the intermingling vibrations of the plant and mineral kingdom.

The crystal receives a constant charge while the plants grow stronger and healthier.

Single points may also be used with the base planted in the soil and the point exposed.

Sleeping with Crystals

It was suggested in Chapter 4 to sleep with your personal crystal, point directed away from the head under a pillow. Its vibrations help in the dream state to guide and direct you on new paths of awareness. In time, as you become more attuned to crystal energies, you will be able to remember more and more of your dreams.

If you have a decision or problem to be worked out, hold the crstal point up in your receptive hand (left for some and right for others) and request a solution be found through the sleep state. On awakening, hold it once more and wait for your consciousness to recall the answer. If nothing immediately comes to mind, then periodically during the day pick up the crystal. The solution is always available if you are willing to search for it.

Crystals may be used in the bed. Many grids and configurations can be made to increase spiritual and physical aspects while you are asleep. One such pattern is given below, but it should not be implemented until you can tolerate crystal energies and understand how the mind and body are affected.

Pattern for Sleeping

This configuration is based on the Star of David to help promote balance between your spiritual and physical growth. Six single points of at least two inches in size, a knife and several feet of copper wire are needed. The actual length of the wire will vary depending on the size of the bed.

The crystals and copper grid can be put between the mattress and box springs, but the metallic materials in the springs can interfere with the effectiveness of the quartz. Also, the copper wiring will not be secure unless tacked onto the box springs. A better solution would be to use a two-inch piece of foam which is laid directly on top of the mattress. This will allow you to cut out the foam for precise placement of the crystal pattern. You will also receive more benefits from the grid as you will be sleeping directly on top of the configuration. Directions for cutting and placement of such is explained below.

Foam Grid System

1. Measure your mattress and obtain a piece of foam to exactly fit on top of the bed. Use a knife and begin to slit the foam about one inch in depth, three inches from the outside of the material. Cut around the foam, rounding the four corners. The finished slit will be lightly oblong in shape. The diagram will assist you.

2. Place the copper wire inside the cut. You need to create a complete circuit of energy, so make sure the wire is long enough to insert.

3. You then program the crystals for protection, to maximize spiritual growth, recall dreams or whatever

CUTTING THE FOAM

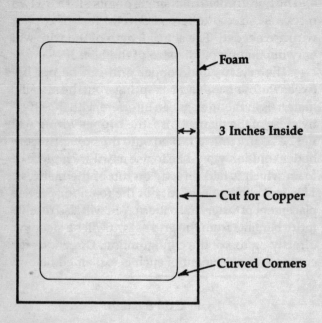

→ **Foam**

←→ **3 Inches Inside**

← **Cut for Copper**

← **Curved Corners**

change you wish to effect. Wrap each with a piece of copper wire as close to the middle as possible with at least three turns of copper. Leave the ends of the wire free (refer to instructions for wrapping crystals on page 167 in Chapter 10). The finished wrapping will look like this:

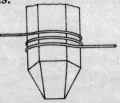

Copper Wire

4. The first crystal is placed with its point falling in a clockwise direction and inserted into the foam's wiring. Take the loose ends of the crystal wires and entwine them around the copper in the foam. This crystal needs to go in the center of the head of the foam with its point directed to the right (see diagram). The second will fall approximately at shoulder level (when you are lying down), and is secured in the same manner as the previous crystal. The third goes at the ankle area, pointed toward the foot of the foam. The fourth is in the center of the bottom of the foam with the point going to the left. The fifth and sixth are opposite the ankle and shoulder with the point directed up toward the head.

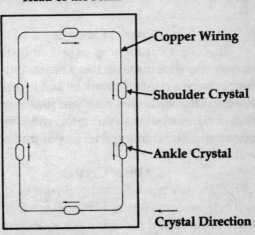

Head of the Foam

Copper Wiring

Shoulder Crystal

Ankle Crystal

Crystal Direction

Foot of the Foam

SLEEPING PATTERN

5. Cover the foam with bedding.

6. Use a generator crystal to connect the energies in a clockwise direction before retiring.

7. Cleanse and energize the crystals at least every two weeks.

This pattern should be used with caution. If you sleep with a partner, ensure that s/he has been exposed to extensive crystal energies and also desires to raise his/her levels of awareness. This formation will bond and unite both your energies together because you are both in the same force field. This arrangement can help smooth over and also bring to conscious realization any difficulties in the relationship. Thus, it is recommended that your sleeping partner be fully alerted to what will occur.

Special Linkages

If you are vacationing or just enjoy the vibrations of a special place such as a beach, mountain or forest, bury a cluster, chunk or single point there. Program it to be linked with you so that in meditation or times of stress, your mind will join with the crystal and the calming energies of that location.

Office Crystals

Place any type of quartz on your office desk. It will help to eliminate negative energies from around the work area and serve as a reminder of your new path of development.

The inner self does not switch off when outside the sanctuary of the home. A balance between all parts of your life needs to be maintained in order for you to function as a complete spiritual and physical being. Remember to cleanse and recharge this crystal at regular intervals.

Telepathy

Crystals can be used to increase your innate powers of telepathy. Being either the receiver or sender exercises the pineal gland associated with the third eye center. Directions are:

1. You and a partner each hold a personal or any single point crystal while sitting directly across from one another.

2. Allow yourselves to relax and drift into a semi-meditative state (one where you are still aware of what is transpiring around you).

3. Decide who will send. Open both your third eye chakras.

4. Begin with simple prearranged symbols such as triangles, circles and squares. The sender points the crystal out at a 90-degree angle from her/his third eye (see following diagram). The receiver points his/her crystal into the third eye.

5. The symbol is mentally visualized as escaping from the third eye opening and traveling over to the receiver's crystal.

6. After a few seconds, the receiver should be able to "see" the symbol.

This exercise can also be used if both partners

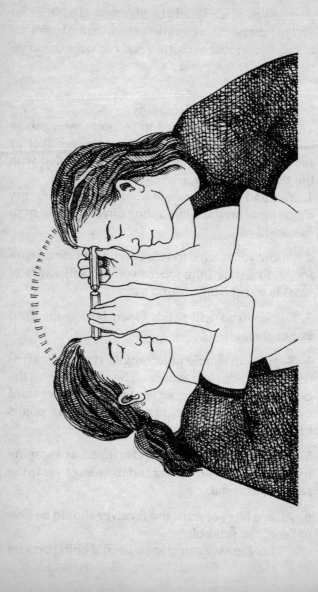

are wearing a crystal headband. The copper will amplify the sender's and receiver's energy, thereby enhancing the process.

With practice and patience, telepathy will begin to happen. After simple symbols have been mastered, move onto colors, emotions and thoughts. There will come a time when the crystal amplification is not needed because the third eye will be fully activated to receive and send, whether or not a partner is sitting directly across from you or on the other side of the globe.

Summary

In order to function in this rapidly changing world, mankind needs to find more peace and harmony within himself. We are just beginning to recognize the potential of crystals to heighten the spiritual and physical aspects of our newly awakened awareness.

Explore within by using the energies of crystals to find total peace and harmony. It is all there, waiting for you.

Footnotes

Chapter 2

1. Rodney Collin, *The Theory of Celestial Influence* (Boulder: Shambhala Publishing House, 1984), p. 49.

2. Katrina Raphaell, *Crystal Enlightenment* (New York: Aurora Press, 1984), p. 55.

Chapter 3

1. William David, *The Harmonics of Sound, Color and Vibration* (Marina del Rey: DeVorss and Company, 1984), p. 43.

2. *Ibid.*, p. 45.

Chapter 4

1. Wally and Jenny Richardson, Lenora Huett, *Spiritual Value of Gemstones* (Marina del Rey: DeVorss and Company, 1985), p. 140.

Chapter 7

1. Vera Stanley Alder, *The Finding of the Third Eye* (New South Wales: Hutchinson, 1938), p. 148.

2. C.W. Leadbeater, *The Chakras* (London: The Theosophical Publishing House, 1927), p. 4.

3. Vera Stanley Alder, *The Finding of the Third Eye*, p. 132.

4. Melita Denning and Osborne Phillips, *Creative Visualization* (St. Paul: Llewellyn Publications, 1985), p.12.

Chapter 8

1. Frank Alper, *Exploring Atlantis Volume 1* (Phoenix: Arizona Metaphysical Society, 1982), p. 36.

Bibliography

Alder, Vera Stanley. *The Finding of the Third Eye*, Broadway, New South Wales: Hutchinson Group, 1938, 1982.

Alper, Frank. *Exploring Atlantis Volumes 1, 2, & 3*, Phoenix, Arizona: Arizona Metaphysical Society, 1982.

Audubon Society, The. *Field Guide to North American Rocks and Minerals*, New York: Alfred A. Knopf Inc. 1979.

Bonewitz, Ra. *Cosmic Crystals*, Whitstable, Kent: Whitstable Litho Ltd., 1983.

Butler, W.E. *The Aura*, Northamptonshire: The Aquarian Press, 1985.

Collin, Rodney. *The Theory of Celestial Influence*, Boulder: Shambhala Publications Inc., 1971.

DaEl. *The Crystal Book*, Sunol, California: The Crystal Company, 1985.

David, William. *The Harmonics of Sound, Color and Vibration*, Marina del Rey, California: DeVorss and Company, 1984.

Encyclopedia Americana Volume 18, Grolier Incorporated, 1981.

Kunz, George Frederick. *The Curious Lore of Precious Stones*, New York: Dover Publications Inc., 1971.

Leadbeater, C.W. *The Chakras*, London, England: The Theosophical Publishing House, 1927.

Matter, Life Science Library. New York: Time, Inc., 1968.

Raphaell, Katrina. *Crystal Enlightenment*, New York: Aurora Press, 1984.

Richardson, Wally and Jenny, Huett, Lenora. *Spiritual Value of Gemstones*, Marina del Rey, California: DeVorss and Company, 1985.

STAY IN TOUCH

On the following pages you will find listed, with their current prices, some of the books now available on related subjects. Your book dealer stocks most of these, and will stock new titles in the Llewellyn series as they become available. We urge your patronage.

To obtain a FREE COPY of our latest full CATALOG of New Age books, tapes, videos, products and services, just write to the address below. In each 80-page catalog sent out bimonthly, you will find articles, reviews, the latest information on New Age topics, a listing of news and events, and much more. It is an exciting and informative way to stay in touch with the New Age and the world. The first copy will be sent free of charge and you will continue receiving copies as long as you are an active customer. You may also subscribe to *The Llewellyn New Times* by sending a $7.00 donation ($20.00 for overseas). Order your copy of *The Llewellyn New Times* today!

The Llewellyn New Times
P.O. Box 64383-Dept. 1058 St. Paul, MN 55164

TO ORDER BOOKS AND PRODUCTS ON THE FOLLOWING PAGES:

If your book dealer does not carry the titles listed on the following pages, you may order them directly from Llewellyn. Please send full price in U.S. funds, plus $3.00 for postage and handling for orders *under* $10.00; $4.00 for orders *over* $10.00. There are no postage and handling charges for orders over $50. Postage and handling rates are subject to change. UPS Delivery: We ship UPS whenever possible. Delivery guaranteed. Provide your street address as UPS does not deliver to P.O. Boxes; UPS to Canada requires a $50 minimum order. Allow 4-6 weeks for delivery. Orders outside the USA and Canada: Airmail—add retail price of book; add $5 for each non-book item (tapes, etc.); add $1 per item for surface mail. You may use your major credit card to order these titles by calling 1-800-THE-MOON, M-F, 8:00-5:00, Central Time. Send orders to:

LLEWELLYN PUBLICATIONS
P.O. BOX 64383-058
St. Paul, MN 55164-0383, U.S.A.

Prices subject to change without notice.

THE MESSAGE OF THE CRYSTAL SKULL
By Alice Bryant & Phyllis Galde

The most fascinating, mysterious artifact ever discovered by mankind. Thousands of years old, yet it is beyond the capabilities of today's technology to duplicate it. Those who have touched the skull or seen photographs of it claim increased psychic abilities and purification. Read this book and discover how this mystical quartz crystal skull can benefit you and all of humankind. Famed biocrystallographer Frank Dorland shares his research of the skull.

0-87542-092-3, mass market, 200 pages, illus., photos $3.95

CRYSTAL SPIRIT
by Michael G. Smith

Crystal Spirit is the book thousands of people have asked for after reading the popular *Crystal Power* by the same author. Now that the fad appeal of crystals is wearing off, we can use crystals to experience the deeper essence of ourselves—to facilitate self-awareness, self-growth, and self-understanding.

Crystal Spirit contains timely and hard-to-find information on:
- New types of crystal rods
- Crystal pyramid devices
- The crystal pipe from Native American traditions
- Ki and Chi energy through crystals for martial artists
- Health and exercise with crystal wristbands

The book begins with explanations of crystals of the ancient past and how to reconstruct your own: the Trident Krystallos, Atlantean Crystal Cross, Crux Crystallum. The book ends with the introduction of the new crystal pipe based on traditional Native American practices and the science of Universal Energy. The crystal pipe, which came into being during the Harmonic Convergence of 1987, is a new tool for the beginning of a new earth cycle. Between these two chapters is a wealth of information and instruction on other crystal inventions, all of which are inexpensive and simple to construct and use, that are beneficial for earth healing and individual development.

0-87542-726-X, 208 pgs., mass market, illustrated $3.95

THE WOMEN'S BOOK OF HEALING
by Diane Stein

This book teaches alternative healing theory and techniques and combines them with crystal and gemstone healing, laying on of stones, psychic healing, laying on of hands, chakra work and aura work, and color therapy. It teaches beginning theory in the aura, chakras, colors, creative visualization, meditation, health theory and ethics with some quantum theory. 46 gemstones plus clear quartz crystals are discussed in detail, arranged by chakras and colors.

0-87542-759-6, 352 pgs., 6 x 9, illus., softcover $12.95

CUNNINGHAM'S ENCYCLOPEDIA OF CRYSTAL, GEM & METAL MAGIC
by Scott Cunningham

Here you will find the most complete information anywhere on the magical qualities of more than 75 crystals and gemstones as well as several metals. The information includes:

The Energy of Each Gem, Crystal or Metal; The Planet(s) Which Rule(s) the Crystal, Gem or Metal; The Magical Element Associated with the Gem, Crystal or Metal; The Deities Associated with Each; The Tarot Card Associated with Each; The Magical Powers each Crystal, Metal and Stone is believed to possess. Also included is a complete description of how to use each gemstone, crystal and metal for magical purposes.

0-87542-126-1, illus., 8 color plates, soft-cover $12.95

SISTER MOON LODGE
Kisma K. Stepanich

Shamanic powers lie dormant in a very natural part of woman's physiology. Through reclaiming and recreating the honor and dignity of the menstrual cycle, women can get in touch with the goddess within, and begin to take part in a greater vision of balance and harmony. Collectively, women can heal the deep wounds that continue to foster weakness in their ideas, creativity and attitudes about being a woman. Includes prayers, poetry, celebrations and rituals.

0-87542-767-7, 272 pp., 6 x 9 softcover $14.95

Prices subject to change without notice.

CRYSTAL POWER
by Michael G. Smith

This is an amazing book, for what it claims to present—with complete instructions and diagrams so that YOU can work them yourself—is the master technology of ancient Atlantis: psionic (mind-controlled and life-energized machines) devices made from common quartz crystals!

Learn to easily construct an "Atlantean" Power Rod that can be used for healing or a weapon; or a Crystal Headband stimulating psychic powers; or a Time and Space Communications Generator; operated purely by your mind.

These crystal devices seem to work only with the disciplined mind power of a human operator, yet their very construction seems to start a process of growth and development, a new evolutionary step in the human psyche that bridges mind and matter.

0-87542-725-1, 288 pgs., illus., 5¼ x 8, softcover $9.95

CRYSTAL HEALING: The Next Step
by Phyllis Galde

Discover the further secrets of quartz crystal! Now modern research and use have shown that crystals have even more healing and therapeutic properties than has been realized. Learn why polished, smoothed crystal is better to use to heighten your intuition, improve creativity and for healing.

Learn to use crystals for reprogramming your subconscious to eliminate problems and negative attitudes that prevent success. Here are techniques that people have successfully used—not just theories.

This book reveals newly discovered abilities of crystal now accessible to all, and is a sensible approach to crystal use. *Crystal Healing* will be your guide to improve the quality of your life and expand your consciousness.

0-87542-246-2, 224 pgs., illus., mass market format $3.95

THE LLEWELLYN ANNUALS

Llewellyn's MOON SIGN BOOK: Approximately 400 pages of valuable information on gardening, fishing, weather, stock market forecasts, personal horoscopes, good planting dates, and general instructions for finding the best date to do just about anything! Articles by prominent forecasters and writers in the fields of gardening, astrology, politics, economics and cycles. This special almanac, different from any other, has been published annually since 1906. It's fun, informative and has been a great help to millions in their daily planning. **State year $4.95**

Llewellyn's SUN SIGN BOOK: Your personal horoscope for the entire year! All 12 signs are included in one handy book. Also included are forecasts, special feature articles, and an action guide for each sign. Monthly horoscopes are written by Gloria Star, author of *Optimum Child*, for your personal Sun Sign and there are articles on a variety of subjects written by well-known astrologers from around the country. Much more than just a horoscope guide! Entertaining and fun the year around. **State year $4.95**

Llewellyn's DAILY PLANETARY GUIDE and ASTROLOGER'S DATEBOOK: Includes all of the major daily aspects plus their exact times in Eastern and Pacific time zones, lunar phases, signs and voids plus their times, planetary motion, a monthly ephemeris, sunrise and sunset tables, special articles on the planets, signs, aspects, a business guide, planetary hours, rulerships, and much more. Large 5-1/4 x 8 format for more writing space, spiral bound to lay flat, address and phone listings, time zone conversion chart and blank horoscope chart.
State year $6.95

Llewellyn's ASTROLOGICAL CALENDAR: Large wall calendar of 48 pages. Beautiful full-color cover and full-color inside. Includes special feature articles by famous astrologers, and complete introductory information on astrology. It also contains a Lunar Gardening Guide, celestial phenomena, a blank horoscope chart, and monthly date pages which include aspects, Moon phases, signs and voids, planetary motion, an ephemeris, personal forecasts, lucky dates, planting and fishing dates, and more. 10 x 13 size. Set in Central time, with fold-down conversion table for other time zones worldwide. **State year $9.95**

Prices subject to change without notice.

LLEWELLYN ORDER FORM
P.O. Box 64383-058, St. Paul, MN 55164-0383

You may use this form to order any of the Llewellyn books or products listed in this publication.

Give Title, Author, Order Number and Price.

_____

_____

_____

_____

Be sure to include $2.00 for postage and handling for the first book, and 50¢ for each additional book. There are no postage and handling charges for orders over $50. Minnesota residents add 6% sales tax. You may charge on your ☐ Visa, ☐ Master Card or ☐ American Express.

Account No._____

Exp. Date_____Phone_____

Signature_____

Name_____

Address_____

City, State, Zip_____

_____

Charge card orders ($15.00 minimum) may call 1-800-THE-MOON during regular business hours. Other questions please call 612-291-1970.

☐ Please send me your FREE CATALOG!